The Colonial Merchantman
# SUSAN CONSTANT
# 1605

Anatomy
of the
Ship

# The Colonial Merchantman
# SUSAN CONSTANT
# 1605

## Brian Lavery

Naval
Institute
Press

Published and distributed in the United States
of America and Canada by the
Naval Institute Press
Annapolis, Maryland 21402

First published in Great Britain 1988 by
Conway Maritime Press Ltd
24 Bride Lane, Fleet Street
London EC4Y 8DR

ISBN  0  87021-583-3

Library of Congress Card No. 88-61602

# Contents

**ACKNOWLEDGEMENTS**
I would like to thank the following individuals and institutions: Jamestown Festival Park for involving me in the project; in particular, Ross L Weeks, Executive Director, and Sara Patton, Director. I would also like to thank Warren Reiss, who recommended me, and Stanley Potter who co-operated with me; the staffs of the National Maritime Museum at Greenwich; the Public Record Office in Chancery Lane, London; the British Library; the London Library, and the Pepysian Library, Magdelene College, Cambridge; Jon Adams, for information on the *Sea Venture* wreck; Susan Sutton, especially for information on the later history of the ship; Brian Rice for comments on naval architecture.

# Introduction

The *Susan Constant* was one of the most important ships in world history. She was the lead ship of the three which founded the colony of Virginia in 1607, and thus established the first successful permanent English-speaking colony in the New World. Though the *Mayflower* is much better known, the *Susan Constant* made her transatlantic voyage thirteen years earlier, and, therefore, can claim to have brought the founding fathers of the United States of America.

My work on the *Susan Constant* began when I was asked by the Jamestown Festival Park to act as historical consultant for a projected replica of the ship. One had already been built in 1956, but is now in poor condition; moreover, advances in underwater archaeology and historical research have made it possible to produce a more accurate replica. This ship is now being built in Virginia, mostly according to the plans in this book, and is intended to sail and to carry passengers. Obviously, safety standards have improved since 1607, and the United States Coastguard regulations have to be taken into account. With this in view, the naval architect Stanley Potter of North Carolina has been employed to do the final design of the ship, based on my plans. Stanley Potter has considerable experience in this field; he has worked with William A Baker (of *Mayflower* replica fame) on several historic ships, and has himself designed the *Elizabeth II*, a replica of one of Raleigh's Roanoke ships.

The Jamestown Festival Park is fully committed to making the replica as historically accurate as possible; however one major change has had to be made in the design, in order to meet modern safety standards. If the ship were built according to the lines shown in this book, it has been calculated that her maximum breadth in midships would be underwater. This would reduce stability and safety quite considerably, and is unacceptable in a modern ship, though it was quite common in the early seventeenth century; a report of 1626 on a number of merchant ships states 'We find that these ships aforesaid, as all other ships in general, do lade the diameter of the breadth to the water, and many under water.' It has been agreed, therefore, to increase the depth in hold of the replica by 18in to improve her stability. This will have very little effect on the ship above water. The plans in this book are the original ones, without the extra 18in in the hold.

This volume is rather different from others in the Anatomy of the Ship series, in that it is not based on the original plans of the ship. Very little is known about the *Susan Constant* of 1605, and the plans in this book are reconstructed from first principles, from various contemporary documents. The book has two main aims: first, to record the work I have done on the new replica (making the information available to anyone who might be interested) and to show that the replica is based on real historic principles. Second, it makes the plans of the ship available to historians, modelmakers, and interested members of the public. Besides being of enormous historical importance, the *Susan Constant* was a typical merchant ship of the early seventeenth century, and such vessels are little recorded.

## THE HISTORY OF THE SHIP

According to evidence given before the High Court of Admiralty in December 1606, the *Susan Constant* was then about a year old, so presumably she was launched late in 1605. Her principal owners were Colthurst, Dapper and Wheatley. The Colthurst family had quite extensive shipping interests, including privateering. There is no information about where she was built, but she was registered in London, and almost certainly built on the River Thames. She was a general cargo ship of 120 tons.

She made at least one voyage to Spain during 1606. Late in that year she was chartered by the Virginia Company for the voyage intended to set up the new colony, along with two smaller ships. While anchored in the River Thames near Limehouse, she was in collision with the *Phillip and Francis* of 100 tons, and this led to a case in the High Court of Admiralty.

She set sail for Virginia soon after, and returned in the middle of 1607. After that, she never went back to Virginia, and reverted to ordinary trading, including a voyage from Bristol to Marseilles in 1615 (HCA 30/857). In 1618 there were reports of a case of piracy against a *Susan Constance* of London (HCA 1/6). This may be related to another report that a ship known as the *Susan Constance* of London was one of those captured by Turkish pirates between 1610 and 1620 (MM vol. 36 pp 69–78); on the other hand, these reports might refer to different ships of the same name. Large parts of the history of the *Susan Constant* are still blank.

## THE VIRGINIA VOYAGE

Serious English interest in the territories of North America had begun in 1585, when an expedition under Sir Walter Raleigh had founded a settlement on Roanoke Island, then considered part of the vast territory of Virginia, but now part of North Carolina. That colony had become isolated during the war with Spain, which began soon afterwards, and its settlers disappeared; their ultimate fate is still something of a mystery. A new Virginia Company was founded in 1606, two years after the end of the Spanish War. It was led by Bartholemew Gosnold and other wealthy backers, and it was given a Royal Charter from King James I. Among the 'gentlemen' involved in the project were Gosnold's relations, Edward Maria Wingfield and Captain John Smith.

For the first settlement, the Virginia Company hired three merchant ships: the *Susan Constant* of 120 tons, the *Godspeed* of 40 tons, and the *Discovery* of 20 tons. The captain of the *Susan Constant*, who was also overall commander of naval activities, was Christopher Newport. He already had vast experience of voyages to the Americas, especially the West Indies; he was an excellent seaman, navigator, and leader.

The expedition set sail from the River Thames in December 1606, and anchored in the Downs, off the Kent coast, to await a favourable wind. Besides the crews, the ships carried 144 colonists – 71 on the *Susan Constant*, 52 on the *Godspeed*, and 21 on the *Discovery*. The three ships were windbound in the Downs through January 1607, where, according to one account in Purchas his Pilgrims (vol XVIII, Ams Press, New York, 1965) 'Wee suffered great storms, but by the skilfulnesse of the Captaine wee suffered no great losse or danger.' Early in February, they sailed down the English Channel, and were off the Canary Islands by about the twenty-first of the month. From there, they picked up the trade winds, which carried them across the Atlantic to reach the West Indies on 23 March. They remained in that area for several weeks, taking on fresh food and allowing men ashore to recover their health. Several men had died during the voyage, and John Smith had been placed in confinement, presumably aboard the *Susan Constant*, for disputing with the other leaders. After that, the ships headed up the North American coast, and landed in Chesapeake Bay on 26 April, after a voyage of more than four months.

Having founded the settlement of Jamestown, and carried out some exploration of the area, Newport set off for England aboard the *Susan Constant* in May. He was to return to Virginia several times, but the *Susan Constant* was not chartered again by the Virginia Company. Of the original 144 colonists, 105 were left behind to maintain the colony; the rest had either died of disease, or decided to return home. Out of these, 36 were gentlemen, and the rest were artisans or servants. The early history of the colony was extremely troubled. There were too many 'gentlemen', who refused to do manual labour and disputed constantly among themselves. The aims were not clear, and relations with the Indians, under their powerful chief Powhattan, were always uneasy. Disease and malnutrition killed the majority of the original settlers, but eventually John Smith emerged as leader, and reorganised the survivors to face their hostile environment. During this period, Smith was almost beaten to death on Powhattan's orders, until the chief's daughter Pocohantas interceded to save him. New supplies of people and goods arrived from England, despite the loss of the *Sea Venture* at Bermuda in 1609. The colony survived, though it was a long time before it became profitable and self-sufficient. Compared with the Puritan colony of New England, founded thirteen years later, the early Virginians appear inept. But they did found English-speaking America, and the oldest of the United States.

## SOURCES

**General:** The general policy has been to recreate the *Susan Constant* from the best possible sources, using all the information available on the ship herself (which is not very much), and otherwise designing her as a typical merchant ship of the early seventeenth century. As far as possible, English sources have been used, because there were certain variations in the ships of different nations – and sources which can be dated within about twenty-five years on either side of 1607 are strongly preferred. Ship design of the period was conservative, and change was slow, but it was not entirely static. It is tempting to rely on much later sources, such as *Deane's Doctrine of Naval Architecture* (B Lavery (ed), Conway Maritime Press, 1981) but these are used mainly to confirm that certain features, such as half beams, had not been invented by 1670, and therefore were unlikely in 1607.

**Archaeological sources:** In the thirty years since the last replica of the *Susan Constant* was built, there have been many notable advances in our knowledge of ships of this period, through both documentary research and underwater archaeology. The two most famous examples of the latter are the *Vasa* in Stockholm, and the *Mary Rose* at Portsmouth. The *Mary Rose* was, of course, an English ship, but she sank sixty years before the *Susan Constant* was built, so I have only used her to a limited extent. The *Vasa* falls within an acceptable time scale, but she was Swedish built to a Dutch design. Nevertheless, she is useful for certain features, such as gun carriages, cook room layout, and pumps, where the information from other sources is scant, and practices seem to have been similar from one country to another. Mostly, the information is taken from a set of plans and photographs published by the *Vasa* Museum in Stockholm.

The wreck of the *Sea Venture* is of course highly relevant. The ship comes from exactly the right place and period, and she was lost off Bermuda in 1609 on the way to Virginia. She was somewhat larger than the *Susan Constant*, but the main difficulty is that only a small proportion of the ship survives underwater; this does, however, provide useful information about structural details of ships of this period. I have used Jon Adams's articles in the *International Journal of Nautical Archaeology*, especially in vol 14, 4; pp 275–99.

**Documentary sources:** Turning to the documentary sources, the most important event was the discovery of the High Court of Admiralty Case of 1606, the documents of which are published in *New American World* (vol V, edited by D B Quinn) and by the Hakluyt Society (Phillip L Babour (ed), *The Jamestown Voyages under the First Charter, 1606–9*, vol 1, 1969). Unfortunately, these say little about the *Susan Constant* herself, beyond establishing the tonnage. One or two other items on the history of the ship have come to light during recent investigations, including some mentions of the ship in the customs records, and a reference to a case of piracy against the *Susan Constance* in 1618.

**Contemporary treatises on naval architecture:** General accounts of the technique of ship design, written between 1585 and about 1625, are very useful. These include:

1 Matthew Baker's so-called *Fragments of Early English Shipwrighty*, in the Pepysian Library, Cambridge. This has still not been published in full, though most of the interesting illustrations can be found in other publications, such as Frank Howard's *Sailing Ships of War*, cited below. There is a photocopy and transcription in the National Maritime Museum at Greenwich, and the original has been consulted for doubtful points. The illustrations are very helpful, but the text has remarkably little real shipbuilding content. Baker, who produced the earliest sections of the text, seems more interested in showing off his knowledge of arithmetic than in providing information on his principles of ship design. Later the book was used as a notebook by others, including John Wells – a dockyard official and mathematician – so the tendency to discuss mathematics rather than naval architecture is reinforced. The other difficulties with this manuscript are that the illustrations tell us much more about the exterior of ships than the basic design – matters such as rigging and decoration changed quite substantially between 1586 and 1607. It also deals mostly with quite large ships, and usually warships rather than merchantmen.

2 Thomas Harriot's notes on shipbuilding, in the British Library. These are of first-class importance for several reasons: because Harriot was a close friend of Raleigh, and sailed to Virginia with him in 1585; because they deal mostly with

merchant ships of around 100 tons, which were similar to the *Susan Constant*; and because they are believed to date from around 1608. The Harriot text has been used in preference to any other source. On the other hand, the text is disarranged and far from complete, and despite attempts to reconstruct it (by Jon V Pepper in *Five Hundred Years of Nautical Science*, published by the National Maritime Museum in 1981), it has many gaps.

3 An anonymous treatise on shipbuilding, believed to have been written around 1625, and published in 1958 by the Society of Nautical Research. This deals with a warship of around 500 tons, but, despite that, it is equal to Harriot in importance, and it fills most of the gaps in that work. Between these two publications there is enough information to attempt a reasonably accurate reconstruction of the shape of the hull. The anonymous document is referred to as 'the Admiralty Library manuscript' in the text which follows. It is combined with a 'Treatise on Rigging' of around the same date in the SNR publication.

One well known document which has not been used is that attributed to George Weymouth in the Scott Library of the Institute of Naval Architects. There are serious doubts about the attribution to Weymouth, and the system of drawing the hull described there is rather later than is generally assumed, and probably dates from the 1640s.

**Nautical dictionaries:** Several nautical dictionaries were written in the quarter century after the founding of Virginia. These are:

1 Mainwaring's Dictionary, probably written in 1623 and published by the Navy Records Society in 1922. It is authoritative, and contains many useful descriptions of shipbuilding techniques and practices, and a great deal of information on other matters.

2 John Smith's *Accidence* and *Sea Grammar*. Smith's personal connection with the *Susan Constant* obviously makes these works essential reading, though the *Accidence* is mostly too vague to be useful, while the additional detail in the *Sea Grammar* is largely copied from Mainwaring. However, it contains some useful new material. For the *Sea Grammar* I have used the edition edited by Kermit Goell and published by Michael Joseph in 1970. The *Accidence* is published in *The Complete Works of Captain John Smith*, edited by P L Barbour, University of North Carolina, 1986.

3 *Boteler's Dialogues*, published by the Navy Records Society in 1929, are of limited value. They were written in the 1630s, and, to some extent, copied from Mainwaring, but with a certain amount of useful additional information.

**Other printed sources:** Several other printed volumes of contemporary manuscripts have been used. *Trinity House Transactions*, published by the London Records Society in 1983, contains much interesting material, particularly about the method of measuring tonnage, and the proportions and fitting of ships. *The Jacobean Commissions of Enquiry*, published by the Navy Records Society in 1971, has some interesting papers. *The Autobiography of Phineas Pett*, published by the Navy Records Society in 1918, has some information on ship design, but Pett is more inclined to name-dropping than detail of shipbuilding. *The Naval Tracts of William Monson* vol IV (Navy Records Society, 1913) also have some useful comments on ship design, but again rather vague. Raleigh's *Works* (Oxford, 1829) includes a few papers of minor usefulness, such as his 'Discourse on the invention of ships' (vol 8 of the *Works*).

**Manuscripts:** Several other unpublished manuscripts have been used, mostly among the State Papers in the Public Record Office at Chancery Lane. The most important of these are:

1 Lists of armament issued to merchant ships, 1625–7. This helped to establish the right number of guns to be carried by a ship of the *Susan Constant*'s size (SP 16/16 no 4).

2 Surveys of ships in the Royal Navy in 1626/7 soon after the accession of Charles I. The most useful is the survey of the *Moon*, of around 100 tons, rebuilt in 1602, as a ship similar in size and date to the *Susan Constant*. Obviously, the *Moon* was a warship, but merchant ships were built to be 'defensible', and ships of over 100 tons received a subsidy from the government so that they could be taken over by the navy in wartime if necessary. The distinction between warships and merchantmen was not nearly so great as in modern times, so it is possible to use the scantlings of the *Moon* as the basis for the *Susan Constant*'s structure, and also for some of the details of her fitting.

3 Surveys of the cook rooms of several ships, including the *Moon*. These tend to confirm that the cook room fitted to the *Vasa* would also be applicable to an English ship.

**Secondary sources:** The more authoritative secondary sources include:

Ralph Davis *Rise of the English Shipping Industry*, 2nd edition, David and Charles, 1972

M Oppenheim *History of the Administration of the Royal Navy*, John Lane the Bodley Head, 1896

R C Anderson *Seventeenth-Century Rigging*, 4th impression, Model and Allied Press, 1974

James Lees *Masting and Rigging of English Ships of War*, Conway Maritime Press, 1979

Frank Howard *Sailing Ships of War*, Conway Maritime Press, 1979 (particularly useful for illustrations)

B Lavery *Arming and Fitting of English Ships of War*, Conway Maritime Press, 1987 (contains much detail on boats, anchors, capstans, guns, steering, etc.)

# GENERAL LAYOUT

## SIZE AND PROPORTIONS

The tonnage of the *Susan Constant* is given in the High Court of Admiralty case of 1606 as 120 tons. This is more likely than the 100 tons given by John Smith in his accounts of the voyage. It seems probable that, by the time he wrote the account, Smith had only a vague memory of the ship, while the evidence at the court was immediate, and was given by professional seamen, during their service as members of the crew. The size of the ship was a material point in the case, and any mis-statement about it would have been challenged by one side or the other.

The tonnage is virtually the only hard information we have specific to the ship, but from this it is possible to find its proportions, using the rules for tonnage measurement. In 1606 the rule was (length of keel × breadth inside the plank × depth from the top of the keel to the height of maximum breadth amidships) divided by 100. It is, therefore, necessary to look at the rules by which these three dimensions were proportioned one to another.

Some writers, including Harriot, suggest that length/breadth/depth should be 1 to 0.4 to 0.2. Baker suggests similar proportions in some parts of his manuscript, though those he quotes from actual ships are rather different:

| Tonnage of ship | Length | Breadth | Depth |
|---|---|---|---|
| 96 | 1 | 0.416 | 0.208 |
| 126 | 1 | 0.423 | 0.219 |
| 100 | 1 | 0.444 | 0.222 |
| 200 | 1 | 0.4 | 0.2 |

As a general rule, Baker suggests that the breadth should be between a half and a third of the length of the keel, and the depth, a half to a third of the breadth; clearly this gives little guidance. The Admiralty Library manuscript (*c* 1625) gives proportions of 1 to 0.4 to 0.166.

Another possibility is to choose the dimensions of a particular ship, preferably a merchantman. The best known of these was the *Adventure of Ipswich*, which was used as an example for devising new tonnage rules in 1627 (Trinity House Transactions, pp 79–80). Her dimensions were:

| | |
|---|---|
| Length of keel | 63ft 6in |
| Breadth | 26ft 2in |
| Depth in hold | 11ft |
| Tonnage | 182.8 |

This gives proportions of 1 to 0.411 to 0.173. Thus the breadth seems to have remained fairly constant from 1586 to 1627, at 0.4 of the length or a little more. The depth seems to have been reduced over the years, from 0.2 in all the earlier manuscripts, to 0.166 or 0.173 in the 1620s. There is no sure way of knowing exactly when the change took place, but the proportions of the *Adventure* are used here, as an example of a known merchant ship of approximately the right period.

Another list of the dimensions of merchant ships is dated 1625 (SP 16/57). Unfortunately, these give the draught of water instead of the depth in hold, so they do not help us much in the controversial matter of depth. Taking the average of these ships gives an average length/breadth ratio of 1 to 0.392, but for the smaller ships on the list (around 200 tons) this is reduced to 0.4167. This is very similar to the proportion of the *Adventure*. The depth in hold of the

*Adventure* is low by most standards, but it is based on the best available information for a ship of the first quarter of the century. Since the depth in hold was equal to half the height of the ship to the toptimber line, this tends to produce a ship with comparatively low topsides, and hence a better sailer.

The basic dimensions are therefore:

| | |
|---|---|
| Length of keel | 55ft 2½in |
| Breadth | 22ft 9in |
| Depth in hold | 9ft 6½in |
| Tonnage | 120 |

## THE BASIC PROFILE (A1)*

It is now necessary to determine the shape of the stem and sternpost of the ship. The sternpost was invariably straight, rising from the after end of the keel. Harriot gives an angle of 22½ degrees to the vertical, Baker gives 70 degrees to the horizontal, while the Admiralty Library manuscript gives 18 to 22 degrees to the vertical. A suitable average is, therefore, 20 degrees to the vertical. The length of the sternpost is determined by the height of the tuck, which is discussed later.

The shape of the stem is determined by a large segment of a circle, known as the 'sweep of the stem'. There is no firm consensus over the years about whether or not this curve should be a tangent to the line of the keel; Matthew Baker provides some drawings in which it forms a tangent with the keel, others in which it clearly does not. However, both Harriot and the Admiralty Library manuscript suggest that it should be tangential to the keel, and these are regarded as the most reliable sources.

Baker gives no information about how to work out the radius of the sweep. Harriot suggests it should be between the breadth and the depth, which is extremely vague. The Admiralty Library manuscript suggests that it should be between the breadth and three quarters of the breadth, but gives 0.791 of the breadth as the best proportion. This has been used, giving a sweep of 16.94ft.

Harriot gives the depth of the keel for a ship of about 100 tons as 12in. This has been used.

## THE POSITIONS OF THE FRAMES (B2)

The midship frame is not exactly in the centre of the ship – according to the Admiralty Library manuscript it should be one third of the length of the keel from the fore edge of the keel, and this has been used. Harriot gives figures for the frame spacings of ships of the appropriate size; for a ship of 22ft breadth, there should be 19in 'room and space', meaning that the distance from a certain point on one frame to the same point on the next frame should be 19in. Following conventional practice, each third frame is used in the lines plans. These are numbered both forward and aft of midships. Harriot also says a ship of this size should have 50 frames, and this approximately agrees with the plan.

In the extreme forward part of the ship the shape becomes more complex, and it is useful to draw out each individual frame, rather than one in three. This is done from frame 18 to 22.

## THE SHEER PLAN – SHAPE OF THE BOW AND STERN (A2)

It is now possible to begin drawing the outboard profile of the ship, using the keel, stempost and sternpost as a basis. According to the Admiralty Library manuscript, the stern post has a height equal to 8/7 of the depth in hold – in other words, it extends upwards for one seventh of the depth above the height

---

* Figures in brackets refer to The Drawings.

of breadth horizontal (horizontal line parallel with the keel at the height of the maximum breadth in midships). Above this, is the counter, which in this plane is represented by a circle tangential to the sternpost. The diameter of the counter is given as 11/10 of the depth. Large ships usually had more than one counter, but this does not seem likely with a ship of the *Susan Constant*'s size.

Above the counter is the flat of the stern, which is here represented by a straight line. None of the documents gives much information on where to place it on the segment of the counter, or on the angle at which it has to be placed. It has been set at an angle rather less than that of the sternpost, because this seems to be usual in the Matthew Baker manuscript. It is best if the join between the counter and the flat of the stern coincides with the after end of the lower deck, and the position of this is discussed later.

In the bows, the sweep of the stem continues until it becomes vertical, ie, until it reaches a level with its own centre. After that it is continued for a short distance with a vertical straight line. The exact height of this line, and also the flat of the stern, depend mainly on the deck arrangement, which is also discussed later.

## PLACING THE LOWER WALE (A3)
According to the Admiralty Library manuscript, the wales are formed in this plane by a segment of a circle. It must pass through three points. The first is the lower edge of the counter, where the sternpost ends. This has already been determined. At the midship frame, it should be at the waterline, according to the Admiralty Library manuscript. According to Harriot, 'a ship of 20ft broad the watermark is counted 1ft under' the maximum breadth, and this gives the midships position. Finally, the Admiralty Library manuscript gives a height of 8/7 of the depth in hold for the forward end of the wale above the keel. A circle, radius 725in, is used to connect these three points. Since the other wales are parallel to this one, the same circle will be used for them later. Harriot gives no specific information on placing the other wales, and the Admiralty Library manuscript is applicable to a much larger ship; therefore it is better to place the upper wales after the positions of the decks and gunports have been calculated. The depth of the lower wale is 9in according to the survey of the *Moon*.

## THE WATERLINE (A3)
The waterline amidships has already been determined while finding the position of the lower wale. Ships of this time were usually 'trimmed by the stern', ie, they were ballasted so that their stern was lower in the water than the bows. There is no detailed information on exactly how this was done, so a rather arbitrary line is drawn as the load waterline. It is necessary to find the line at this stage, as it will be used later in positioning the gunports.

## THE SHAPE OF THE LOWER DECK (A2)
All the evidence suggests that most ships of this period had rises and falls in the decks, and that a single continuous deck throughout the whole length of the ship was quite rare, even in a ship as small as the *Susan Constant*. The *Moon* certainly had such rises and falls, while in the 1620s Mainwaring argues strongly against the use of such rises and falls in warships, implying that they had been common up till then. On the other hand, the Admiralty Library manuscript distinctly favours them: 'to lay the deck flush fore and aft cannot be done without cutting the wales, which is both disgraceful and weakening to the ship' (p 27).

In both the Admiralty Library manuscript and the survey of the *Moon*, it is clear that the deck rises forward and falls aft. The actual sizes of these sections can be calculated from the *Moon*. According to the survey, she had four beams in the forward section (the fore peak), 4ft apart, giving a length of 12ft for that section, or possibly a little more if the deck extended forward of the foremost beam. The after part, in the gunroom, had four beams, also 4ft apart, giving a similar length. There is not enough data to calculate the length of the centre section, the lower deck itself; but the centre section of the upper deck would have had a similar length, and it had seven beams 6ft apart, giving a length of 42ft. Using these proportions for guidance, it is possible to calculate proportions for the decks of the *Susan Constant*. The survey of the *Moon* seems to imply that the falls and rises should be of 12in, and this has been used.

The next task is to find the height of the lower deck in midships. The Admiralty Library manuscript says of this, 'Let the lower edge of the beam for the orlop be pitched at the breadth line' (p 27). (In this period, 'orlop' meant deck in general, not necessarily the light deck under the waterline, as it came to mean later.) Since the position of the deck is to be taken from the top edge of the beam where it meets the side of the ship, it is now necessary to find the thickness of the deck beam; this is 10in, according to the survey of the *Moon*.

The Admiralty Library manuscript states that it is best that 'the gunroom and fore peak lie upon a level, and the deck between camber conveniently to keep the wales whole and to place the ports at equal height above the deck' (p 28). This means that each part of the deck has to be lower at its fore than at its after part.

The distance between the lower and the upper deck is given as 6ft by John Smith (p 17) and also by the Admiralty Library manuscript (p 28). The Admiralty Library manuscript is clearly dealing with a larger ship, but Smith seems to imply that the rule has general application. This does not mean that there is six feet clear between one deck and another, for it is merely the distance between the top edge of one deck beam and the same point on the corresponding beam above – the thickness of the deck planking (2in), and also the thickness of the upper deck beams (6in) have to be subtracted, so that the minimum distance between the decks will be 5ft 4in, and more in the spaces between the beams.

The falls in the upper deck are placed directly above those of the lower deck, and bulkheads are fitted at the falls.

The quarterdeck is placed above the after part of the deck, running from the bulkhead to the stern. At the bulkhead, it is six feet above the deck below, but this is increased towards the stern, to give more room in the captain's cabin. There is no direct evidence that this was normal in the 1600s, but it was certainly common by 1670 – Sir Anthony Deane's time – and the high sterns of ships in contemporary prints seem to suggest that it was common earlier in the century.

A study of the same prints suggests that a poop deck was not likely on a ship this small; furthermore, after the lines are drawn out, it will be seen that a hull designed by this method would be too narrow at the upper stern to allow a suitable cabin under the poop.

Trinity House Transactions has some discussion on stowing the hold of a merchant ship of this period, and it is implied that the norm was three tiers of casks, occupying a total height of 7ft 4in. This fits quite neatly into the hold of the *Susan Constant*, without leaving any room for an orlop deck. However, there ought to be store rooms in the bows, for rigging parts, gunners' stores, spare timber for repairs, etc. In the after hold is the bread room, which is mentioned in the survey of the *Moon*.

## THE MAST POSITIONS (A4)

It is better to determine the positions of the masts at this stage, as it can have some effect on the siting of the gunports, and also on the channels and hence the channel wales. This section is largely based on R C Anderson's *Seventeenth-Century Rigging*.

The mainmast was placed somewhere between the middle of the keel and the middle of the gundeck, tending to move forward over the years. Here, it is placed forward of the middle of the keel. It should be vertical.

The foremast should be just within the forecastle, according to Baker. It should rake 5 degrees or less.

The mizzen, according to Anderson, should be 'nearly as far from the taffrail as from the mainmast'. Baker says about a quarter of the distance from the taffrail to the mainmast. However, in Baker's time it was common to use a small boom extending from the stern, to stretch the foot of the mizzen sail. A study of the prints shows that this boom had largely been abolished by 1600, and after that, the mizzen would tend to move forward. In view of this, the mizzen is placed a third of the distance between the taffrail and the mainmast, as a compromise; but its position was changing quite quickly over the years, and there can be no certainty about this. It should rake about 5 degrees, slightly more than the foremast.

The bowsprit passes through the angle between the forecastle bulkhead and the upper deck. It is offset to one side (starboard) in order to keep out of the way of the foremast. It is angled upwards (steeved). Anderson gives an angle of about 24 degrees for the middle of the seventeenth century, while the ships in Matthew Baker's drawings usually have about 35 degrees. In our case, 30 degrees is used as a compromise.

## THE ARMAMENT (K1–13)

There is no direct information about the guns carried by the *Susan Constant*, but the Public Records contain details of guns carried by merchant ships of a similar size and period. The earliest information on this comes from 1626 (SP 16/16, no 4): a series of papers on guns approved for merchant ships by the government. Ships of around 120 tons mentioned include:

*Ann* of London, 104 tons, 8 minions
*Prissel*? of Yarmouth, 120 tons, 8 minions
*Thomas and George* of London, 104 tons, 8 minions
*Diligence* of Yarmouth, 120 tons, 4 minions, 2 falcons
*Hopewell* of London, 110 tons, 5 falcons and 2 minions

Other ships, from a list of those belonging to the port of Hull:

| | |
|---|---|
| 100 tons | 2 minions |
| 140 tons | 6 minions |
| 120 tons | 6 minions |
| 120 tons | 3 minions |
| 100 tons | 2 minions, 1 falcon |
| 100 tons | 4 minions |
| 140 tons | 6 minions |
| 120 tons | 2 minions, 2 falcons |
| 100 tons | 6 minions |
| 100 tons | 6 minions |
| 100 tons | 6 minions, 4 falcons |
| 100 tons | 6 minions, 2 falcons |
| 100 tons | 4 minions, 3 falcons |
| 100 tons | 6 minions |
| 120 tons | 4 minions, 4 falcons |
| 100 tons | 2 minions, 2 falcons |
| 100 tons | 2 minions, 2 falcons |

Since the *Susan Constant* was clearly fitted out for a voyage involving dangers from Indians and possibly Spanish, it is not unreasonable to assume that she would have quite a heavy armament for her size. Out of the above list, the 120-ton ship third from bottom on the list seems most suitable, as carrying an above-average armament.

Against this, it is worth mentioning that accounts of the early colony say that the colonists had culverins ashore. Since a culverin was a heavier gun than any of those in the above list, it seems likely that they were carried in the holds of the ships as ballast, and mounted later.

Having settled on an armament of eight guns, with four gunports on each side, it is easier to identify ships of a similar size on prints, and this is useful in designing the decoration and rigging of the ship.

## POSITIONING THE GUNPORTS (A5)

The size of the gunports is, to a certain extent, arbitrary. The Admiralty Library manuscript suggests that they should be 2½ft square (p 29), though of course they will be an indeterminate amount smaller on a smaller ship. On the *Susan Constant*, it is necessary to adjust this size so that they fit in well between the timbers. Ideally, a port should begin at the side of one frame, extend through the next one, and end at the side of a third. The room and space is known to be 1ft 7in, so that, over two frames, it should be 3ft 2in. The thickness of the frames at this point is 5½in, according to the survey of the *Moon*, and subtracting that gives a breadth of 2ft 8½in, which is rather larger than the Admiralty Library manuscript figure. However, if it can be assumed that the frames are scarfed at that point, another 5½in can be deducted, leaving the gunport at 2ft 3in, which seems reasonable. Since ports were usually square at that time, the vertical height is also 2ft 3in. However, because of the tumble home of the side, the actual length of the port lid is slightly more.

The Admiralty Library manuscript suggests that the gunports should be 6ft above the waterline. This was a figure which designers dreamed of throughout the ages – in the time of Samuel Pepys, in 1745, and towards the end of the eighteenth century (B Lavery, *Ship of the Line* vol 1, Conway Maritime Press, 1983, pp 37, 91 and 139). It is unlikely that this was ever achieved before the 1800s, when ships were much larger and the camber of the deck was much reduced. Therefore, the ports of the *Susan Constant* are placed somewhat less above the water – about 4ft in midships. To make them any higher would probably put the guns too close to the deck above, and make them difficult to operate.

The four ports have to be distributed fairly evenly along each side – one in the gunroom, one in the fore peak, and two spaced evenly on the main part of the deck. In practice the one in the fore peak has to be as far aft as possible, because otherwise it will be in the way of the bowsprit. This means that on the *Susan Constant* the guns are about 14ft apart.

## THE UPPER WALES (A3)

The wales, apart from the lower one, have to be positioned so that they are cut by the gunports as little as possible, though it is rare to find a ship in which they are not cut to some extent, because the curve of the wales is much greater than that of the decks, especially if falls are used to keep the gunports on a level. The wales which have to be positioned in this way are:

1 The second wale, which is only a short distance above the lower wale, and forms a pair with it (though it is often rather less thick than the lower wale), is 6in deep, according to the survey of the *Moon*.

2 The upper and lower channel wales are substantially thinner than the lower wales. The upper wale helps to support the channels, while the lower one supports the chains which lead down from the channels. Normally, the channels should be at the level of the upper deck, so it is important that the channel wale should be at this level just behind the mast. They are both 5½in deep on the *Moon*.

3 The gunwale in midships is at the height of the toptimber line but, again, the wale curves rather more than the toptimber line, so it rises towards the bow and stern. Nevertheless, the position of the gunwale is established by this.

4 Two rails were used for the forecastle, still parallel to the lower rail. The upper one forms the top of the side, and it is positioned so that it is very slightly above the level of the deck. There is no precise data on the thickness of the wales and rails above the channel wales but, clearly, they should be less than 5½in: say, 4in.

5 Three rails were used for the stern; in order to give the high stern so often seen in prints of the period, the two topmost rails are no longer parallel to the lower wale.

A template was made in the shape of the curve of the lower wale, and moved about parallel to the lower wale, so that the position of each wale could be fixed. Only the second wale has been cut by a gunport, and even this could be avoided if the wale was lowered, or the port raised, or both.

## THE SHAPE OF THE UPPER WORKS

Finding the position of the wales and rails involves some decisions about the shape of the stern and forecastle. The quarterdeck extends all the way to the stern, but the forecastle stops some way short of the bows, to allow a short deck forward of the bulkhead for handling ropes and anchors, and to give access to the heads for sanitary purposes. The forecastle has to end on one of the frames of the hull – in this case on frame 18 – which seems to give a suitable length to both the forecastle and the foredeck.

As explained earlier, the planking of the forecastle ends at a wale which is just above the level of the deck. This is necessary in order to keep the structure of the forecastle reasonably low. In particular, it has to be considerably lower than that of the stern, in order that the ship will come into wind when the sails are down or the masts carried away: this was essential to the design of ships of that period.

Another rail should be fitted above the forecastle, supported by stanchions but not planked over. The height of the stern is largely arbitrary, as none of the texts give any real guidance on how to determine it on a ship of this size. It is not so high as the stern shown on many prints of the period, but perhaps artists and engravers had a tendency to exaggerate the height.

Though a higher stern might tend to make the ship look more like the popular image of a ship of the period, there are good arguments against it. Some of the ships in the Matthew Baker text have quite low sterns, in particular the ship of 200 tons (Photograph 1). The ship in the Admiralty Library manuscript has a stern which is relatively lower than that on the projected *Susan Constant* – 0.226 of the overall length of the ship compared with 0.245 for the *Susan Constant*.

The sides of the hull extend some way forward of the quarterdeck bulkhead, and aft of the forecastle. Again, this is purely arbitrary, and intended to give an appearance more like the ships in the prints.

# HULL FORM

## THE MIDSHIP SECTION (B1)

The midship section, like every other frame in the ship, is made up of a series of straight lines and segments of circles. The bottom part of the midship frame, known as the floor, is a straight horizontal line at the level of the top of the keel. The curve known as the floor sweep forms a tangent to this line, and begins to carry the shape upwards. The floor sweep is tangential to the reconciling sweep, which has a considerably greater radius. That in turn is tangential to the breadth sweep, which has a slightly smaller radius than the floor sweep. As its name implies, the breadth sweep is placed at the maximum breadth of the ship at each individual frame, and carries on a little way above the breadth. It joins the top timber sweep, which is equal to the reconciling sweep in radius.

The breadth of the ship in midships is already known to be 22ft 9in, while the height of the maximum breadth (ie, depth in hold) from the top of the keel is 9ft 6½in. The breadth of the floor is given by Harriot as half the difference between the breadth and the depth. The half floor is therefore 3ft 3¾in.

The radius of the floor sweep is from half to 7/12 of the half breadth, according to Harriot. Using half, gives a radius of 5ft 8¼in. Harriot gives the radius of the breadth sweep as 2/5 of the half breadth, which gives 4ft 6½in. This sweep is carried on above the breadth line, where it will meet the toptimber sweep.

The reconciling sweep can be 17/10 of the half breadth, according to Harriot, or equal to the full breadth, according to the Admiralty Library manuscript. Using Harriot, gives a radius of 19ft 4in. This sweep has to be made tangential to both the breadth and the floor sweep. This completes the curves below the breadth.

The shape above the breadth is largely controlled by the toptimber line. The height of this above the maximum breadth is equal to the depth in hold, which is 9ft 6½in. The narrowing at the toptimber line is one third of the breadth. This produces a point through which the toptimber sweep must pass. It should also be tangential to the breadth sweep, and in radius it is equal to the reconciling sweep. This completes the shape of the midship frame.

## RISING AND NARROWING LINES (B2)

Four lines – the rising and narrowing lines of the floor, the height of breadth line, and the narrowing line of breadth – control the basic shape of the hull, giving the positions for the sweeps which form the shape of each individual frame along the length of the ship. The 'floor' is a flat area in the lower part of the ship, formed by the timbers, or ribs. Except in midships, this floor is purely theoretical, for as the 'rising line of the floor', or lower rising line, ascends towards the bow and stern, it rises well above the keel, to which it is joined by another line, usually a reverse curve. Furthermore, the 'narrowing line of the floor', or lower narrowing line, narrows so quickly that it crosses the centre line of the ship well before reaching the bow or the stern, so that the floor sweep serves only to guide the 'reconciling sweep', which joins it to the breadth sweep.

The lower rising line is at the level of the upper edge of the keel in midships. Aft, it meets the sternpost at the tuck. For this, Harriot gives a height of half or 5/9 of the depth in hold; 5/9 is used. Forward, it passes through the gripe, which is a point just above the forward end of the keel. According to Harriot, the height of the gripe is 1/5 of the height of the tuck. The shape of the rising line is a circle, which must pass through these three points, and is carried forward from the gripe until it meets the stempost. The radius of this circle is calculated to be 1539.8in.

The upper rising line, or rising line of breadth, is also formed by a circle. In midships it is tangential to a horizontal line drawn at the level of the height of breadth line in midships. Aft, it meets the sternpost at a height of 4/3 of the depth in hold, and forward at 9/8 of the depth in hold (Admiralty Library manuscript). The circle has a radius of 1907.8448in. The toptimber rising line is parallel to the upper rising line, at a distance equal to the depth in hold.

The lower narrowing line is the most difficult to understand. As it was conventionally drawn at that time, it began in midships at half the half breadth, and narrowed to meet the keel aft at the tuck, and forward where the lower rising line meets the stempost. Forward of midships, the line does not narrow for the first four frames, then it narrows in a quartic curve. Aft, it begins to narrow immediately, by means of a cubic curve. The lower narrowing line serves to measure the distance of the floor sweep in each frame inboard from the position of the floor on the midships frame – it does not represent the real position of the floor at any place in the ship.

The midships position of the upper narrowing line is determined by the maximum breadth. Aft, it narrows to meet the wing transom, which is at the top of the sternpost. The breadth of the wing transom is half the breadth in midships, and the narrowing line reduces by a cubic curve, as with the lower narrowing line. Forward of midships, the upper narrowing line is also similar to the lower line, in that it narrows by a cubic curve, but only after the first four frames.

The hull at the toptimber narrowing line has a breadth equal to 2/3 of that at the breadth line. However, this does not work in the area of the forecastle, because the upper hull has to be much broader in that area. Therefore an arbitrary curve is used, to ensure that at the forward end of the forecastle (frame 18) the hull is almost as wide at the toptimber as at the maximum breadth.

## DRAWING OUT THE FRAMES (B3, B4)

Using the data given by the rising and narrowing lines and by the midship section, it is now possible to draw out the form of the hull, taking each frame in turn. The height of the floor is taken from the lower rising line. The breadth of the floor is determined by finding the distance that the lower narrowing line has moved in from its midships position, and measuring that off from the end of the floor in midships. This means that in practice, from frame 21 aft and frame 15 forward, the floor is purely theoretical, as it is all on the wrong side of the centreline.

The centre of the floor sweep is found by drawing a vertical line on the outboard end of the floor. The floor sweep, like all the other sweeps, has the same diameter throughout the length of the ship (this is one of the main ways in which the system, used in the early part of the century, differs from that used later; for example, according to Anthony Deane in 1670, the sweeps generally get narrower towards the bow and stern, giving the naval architect much greater flexibility).

The breadth sweep can be placed by the use of the upper narrowing and rising lines, as with the midship frame. The reconciling sweep and the toptimber sweep are also located as in midships, and it should be noted that the toptimber sweep must pass through the toptimber line in each case. After that, it is extended by means of a straight line tangential to the toptimber line, until it reaches the height prescribed by the sheer draught.

By frame 6 forward or aft, the floor is several inches above the keel, and must be joined to it in some way. Ideally, this should be done by means of a reverse curve of the same diameter as the floor sweep, and this is the case in frames 9–12 forward and 9–15 aft. Closer to midships, this is geometrically difficult, as it will tend to produce an awkward shape, so a French curve is used. Forward of frame 12, the frame has to meet the stempost rather than the keel, and it has to alter from concave at frame 12 to convex by frame 19. Straight lines are used for some of the intervening frames.

Aft of frame 15, the floor is high above the keel, and it is difficult to join it to the keel by means of a single segment. Therefore, French curves are used again to produce a suitable shape. After 23, the frame joins the sternpost rather than the keel, and after 27, it joins the transom.

## THE WATERLINES (B5, B6)

Waterlines are drawn at suitable heights throughout the hull, to give the shape, and particularly to check if the lines are fair. A few small alterations were necessary in the lower part of the hull, in the area below the floor itself. Sometimes, straight lines have to be substituted for curves, but, in general, the lines are surprisingly fair, and the part of the hull designed by means of the sweeps needed no alteration. Contemporary shipwrights did not use waterlines in their drawings, but faired the ship after the frame was set up, trimming off any excess timber with an adze. Because of this, the lines could vary from the plan by an inch or two in places.

## THE SINEMARKS (B5)

The sinemarks, or surmarks, indicate the places where one section of the timber ends and another begins. They are needed by the shipwright in cutting out the hull timbers, and also serve to place the thicker pieces of internal planking which cover the joins of the timbers. Each sinemark is a straight line on the body plan. They are placed according to the instructions in the Admiralty Library manuscript (pp 34–5), though these are sometimes a little obscure. The most important of the sinemarks is the first one, which marks the 'runghead', or end of the floor timbers (presumably it was so called because the structure of the keel with the floor timbers fitted across it looked rather like a ladder). According to the Admiralty Library Manuscript, it is placed at the end of the floor timber. It cannot be drawn as a straight line if this is followed too literally, but it has been drawn as near as possible to the head of the floor timbers. Similar practices have been used in drawing out the other sinemarks.

# STRUCTURE

## THE KEEL (C1, C2, C3)

According to Harriot, a ship of 100 tons should have a keel 10in broad and 12in deep. This figure is used, though the *Susan Constant* is slightly larger. The keel is the same width throughout the length, as suggested by Harriot, though there is some evidence that it should taper towards the ends. This seems to be the case with the keel of the *Sea Venture*. An alternative plan would be to have the keel 12in square in midships, tapering to 10in wide at each end. Certainly the keel should retain the same depth throughout its length.

None of the contemporary sources makes any mention of a false keel, so we can assume that it was not in use at this time.

The forepart of the keel is scarfed into the stempost. The after part should end in a skeg. Instead of ending in line with the sternpost, the lower edge should run further aft than the upper edge, ending the keel at an angle of about 45 degrees. This method is illustrated by Harriot, and described in all the nautical dictionaries. A keel of this size would probably be made in two or three pieces, scarfed together.

The keel is square in section throughout its length, except that a triangular groove, known as the rabbet (a corruption of rebate) is cut along its length on each side, to receive the edge of the lowest plank. The rabbet is just under the top edge of the keel. Its actual shape varies in accordance with the shape of the frame above. In midships, the plank approaches the keel horizontally, while towards the stern it becomes increasingly vertical at each frame. This is partly illustrated in the cross-sections of the ship.

## THE STERNPOST (C4)

The sternpost rises from the after end of the keel at an angle of 20 degrees. Its lower end is tenoned into the keel. Where it meets the keel, it is exactly the same width as the keel (10in). It should get slightly wider as it rises, to perhaps 15in. There is no definite information on the fore and aft size of the sternpost, so a rather arbitrary figure has been chosen. The sternpost should rise as far as the tuck, which is also on a level with the gundeck. Like the keel it is rabbetted to receive the plank, and again the shape of the rabbet varies according to the angle at which the plank approaches the rabbet.

## THE DEADWOOD (A4)

The angle between the keel and the sternpost is largely filled by the deadwood. This is probably made up of several pieces of timber scarfed together, and its upper edge is defined by the lower edge of the kelson. The deadwood is cut out to receive the ends of the half frames which form the hull in this area.

## THE STEMPOST (A3)

The stempost is curved, with a depth equal to that of the keel. It starts off equal to the keel in width, but it becomes slightly wider as it rises, perhaps reaching a width of 15in at its uppermost part. It is probably made in two or three pieces scarfed together, as it would be very difficult to find a single timber with enough curve. The stempost is also rabbetted.

## THE DEADWOOD AND FALSE STEMPOST (A4)

The stempost is backed up with deadwood in its lower part, to receive half frames. It is less deep than that of the stern, because the frames of the bow rise less steeply. As it rises above a certain level, it becomes the false stempost, which holds no half frames, but receives the deck hooks and breast hooks, and gives extra strength to the bows.

## FITTING THE FRAMES

Between station 14 aft and 11 forward, each frame is placed over the top of the keel and bolted. Forward and aft of these positions, the timbers rise steeply, so that a single timber with a suitable grain could not be found. Therefore, half frames were used, fitted into the side of the deadwood. In the extreme part of the bows, hawse pieces, running fore and aft instead of athwartships, were used. These would probably begin at about frame 19 or 20.

## THE THICKNESS OF THE FRAMES (C1, C2, C3)

The frames tend to taper as they rise above the level of the keel, so that the sides of the hull become thinner. Harriot suggests that the thickness at the lowest part should be 8in, and 3in at the upper end. The survey of the *Moon* is more detailed, and gives the following figures:

At the kelson, 8 in
2½ft above the runghead, 5in
At the gunports, 4½in

These two are combined in drawing out the timbers of the *Susan Constant*.

## THE KELSON (C2)

The kelson fits above the frames directly above the keel, to lock them in position. It continues forward and aft over most of the deadwood. The kelson of the *Moon* was 11½in broad and 6in deep, and I have used these dimensions. It is probably made of several pieces scarfed together.

## TRANSOMS (C4)

Transoms are crosspieces running athwartships to form the structure of the counter. Five are used: one supporting the after part of the upper deck and known as the deck transom; one above; one below the tiller where it passes through the counter; one at the level of the lower deck, also known as a deck transom; and another at the lowest part of the counter. There is also another, lighter transom to form the after edge of the bread room platform. There is no information on the dimensions of the transoms, but probably they should be similar to the deck beams in scantling, or perhaps slightly more.

## THE FASHION PIECE (C4)

Each outer edge of the counter is formed by a curved timber known as a fashion piece. The two fashion pieces are joined by the transoms, and to a certain extent they help to support them. Again, there is no detailed information on scantlings, but in thickness they are similar to the frame timbers at the appropriate height. Fore and aft, they should match the transoms which are fixed to them.

## THE FRAMING OF THE STERN (C4)

Above the fashion piece, a straight timber extends diagonally, forming the corner of the extreme stern. Its scantling is similar to that of the frames. Obviously, the last few frames, just forward of the stern timbers, will have their lower ends in the stern timbers or fashion pieces.

The after face of the stern is framed by three or four light timbers running almost parallel to the stern timbers. The stern of a ship of this period was notoriously weak because of this form of construction.

## GUNPORT CILLS (A5)

The gunports are placed so that the vertical edges are formed by hull timbers. The horizontal edges of the ports are formed by cills, one upper and one lower. Each cill runs between the appropriate frames, and is shaped at the end to fit into a triangle cut into the frame. Obviously, the cill has to be as thick as the frame at the appropriate point; in depth, it is probably somewhat less than the thickness of the timber. Other holes in the side of the hull, in particular the windows and doors of the stern cabins, are formed in the same way.

## INTERNAL PLANKING OF THE HOLD

The interior of the hold is planked almost completely, except perhaps for the spaces between the deck beams. Thicker planks, known as sleepers, are placed over the joins in the frame timbers (whose positions can be found by the sinemarks, as described on p 14). The runghead has a particularly thick sleeper, with a slightly thinner plank on each side. According to the survey of the *Moon*, the main runghead sleeper should be 5in thick, with a 4in one next to that, and smaller, 3in, ones on each side. The second sinemark, at the join of the first and third futtock, should have 3in plank. However, the second row of sleepers will eventually merge with the clamp above it.

The clamp is 4in thick and 14in deep. It is placed immediately under the line of the deck beams, to help support them.

The spaces between the clamps and sleepers are filled with 1½in plank. Probably, the strake next to the kelson is removable, to allow access to the frames for cleaning out the limber holes. In later years, this strake was placed diagonally with one edge resting on the top of the kelson, but there is no evidence that this was done in the early seventeenth century.

## THE DECK BEAMS (C5, C6)

In general, the scantlings of the *Moon* are used for the deck beams. For the lower deck these are:

| | |
|---|---|
| Beams, up and down | 10in |
| Beams, fore and aft | 11in |
| Distance between the beams | 4ft |

Harriot suggests that the deck beams should camber ½in for every foot of half breadth. This gives 5¾in for the lower deck.

In two cases, the spacing of the deck beams has to be altered to give room for certain fittings. There is a large main hatch forward of the mainmast. This has to be large enough to let in a butt, 4½ft long (Trinity House Transactions). Such a hatch has to span two beams to be large enough. According to *Deane's Doctrine* of 1670, curved beams and half beams were not yet in use, so one beam has simply been omitted, as in the *Doctrine*.

Forward, a wider space is also left where the bowsprit passes through the upper deck. It does not pass through the lower deck, but the beams have been arranged so that one on the upper deck is directly above one on the lower deck, which means that the space has to be repeated on the lower deck.

The upper deck beams of the *Moon* were 6in square. As already stated, the beams of the *Susan Constant* have been placed directly above those of the lower deck. They have also been given a camber to make them parallel to the lower deck beams.

The beams of the forecastle and quarterdeck have also been placed directly above their counterparts. There is no data on dimensions, but they are made 5in square, slightly less than those of the lower deck. The upper deck, quarterdeck and forecastle do not have to carry guns, so it is quite possible to make the deck beams considerably lighter than those of the lower deck.

## CARLINES (C3, C5, C6, E3)

Carlines are small beams placed between the deck beams proper, with the ends of the carlines dovetailed into the main beams. It was normal to have two rows of carlines on each side of the deck. The innermost one would also help define the outside of the hatches, mast and capstan partners, etc, running down the centreline of the deck, and this has to be borne in mind when deciding the position of the row. They are arranged so that the main hatch would be big enough to take a butt 2ft 8in in diameter, as discussed earlier, with some room to spare. The outer row is placed halfway between the inner row and the side of the ship.

The line of carlines has to be interrupted occasionally, to form partners of the bowsprit on the lower deck, and to allow it to pass through the upper deck; in the extreme forepart of the upper deck, where it is not wide enough for two rows, for example.

The dimensions of the carlines of the *Moon* are used: lower deck, 6in fore and aft by 7½in broad; upper deck, 4in up and down, 6in broad. There are no carlines on the quarterdeck or forecastle.

## THE KNEES (A4, C5)

There are two kinds of knees: hanging and lodging. The lodging knees are set in the same plane as the deck, with one to each deck beam, filling the angle between it and the side of the ship. Forward of midships, the knee is aft of the beam; and aft of midships, it is forward of it. It is convenient to reverse the direction of the beams at the main hatch, where a beam is missed out, and this is how it is done in *Deane's Doctrine*. The knees are roughly L-shaped, with variations to suit particular locations, and with the internal angle left rounded. There is no contemporary information on the sizes of the knees, but they should be slightly thinner than the deck beams, with one arm extending to the row of carlines, and the other going as far as the hanging knee of the adjacent beam.

The hanging knees are placed below the deck, forming an angle between the deck beam and the side of the ship in the vertical plane, with the top edge of the horizontal arm of the L on a level with the upper deck beam. Their position is the converse of that of the lodging knee – before the beam in the foremost part of the ship, and after it in the after part of the ship. Their dimensions are similar to the lodging knees, though it is possible that in midships, where the distance is greater, the beam will not extend as far as the carlines.

Standards are similar to hanging knees, except that they are placed above the deck instead of below. They are not mentioned by either Smith or Mainwaring, so they are not used.

## LEDGES (C3, C5, C6, E3)

Ledges are small timbers placed between the carlines, running parallel to the deck beams, and dovetailed into the carlines. The sizes are given in the survey of the *Moon*: lower deck, 3in up and down and 4in breadth, upper deck, 3in square. The spacings are also given: 10in for the lower deck, and 9in for the lower. Obviously, this requires some local modifications, but in general it works out quite well. The outermost ends of the carlines are dovetailed into the lodging knees.

## DECK HOOKS AND BREAST HOOKS (A3)

Breast hooks are large curved pieces placed in the bows of the ship, inside the frames and planking, to give extra strength. Deck hooks are similar, but are placed at the level of decks in order to support their ends. There is a deck hook at the lower deck, and another for the upper deck, with one breast hook between, and another below. Again, there is no specific information on size, but they are similar to the deck beams, or slightly larger. The lower part of the bow is strengthened by the step of the foremast, which is described later.

## STEPS OF THE FOREMAST AND MAINMAST

The foremast and mainmast steps are curved pieces designed to fit into the hold, inside the frames and internal planking, rather like riders or deck hooks. Each has a flat section in the middle, cut out with a square tenon to receive the step of the appropriate mast. They also serve to strengthen the hull, and should have scantlings similar to the breast hooks, or slightly more.

## PARTNERS (G3, G7)

Partners are used to support important items, such as masts and capstans. They are thick pieces of board, thicker than the deck plank. Each one is bolted to the deck beams forward and aft of the mast or capstan, and also to the carlines on each side. A hole is cut in the middle to allow the mast or capstan to pass through. In the case of a mast, the hole is a few inches wider than the mast. After the mast has been fitted, the space is filled with wedges to keep it tight. Then it might be covered with canvas to keep the water out. The partners of the capstan were perhaps made in two pieces, so that one could be removed to fit the capstan.

## INTERNAL PLANKING OF THE SIDES

The first plank above the deck beams is called the waterway. It forms the join between the side planking and the deck planking, and in a sense it is part of the latter rather than the former. However, it follows the shape of the side of the hull, rather than the strakes of deck planking, which are parallel. It is five sided, with a diagonal section between the deck and side planking. The scuppers run through the waterways. There is no detailed information on the exact size, but it must be thicker than the deck plank.

The first section of ordinary planking is called the spirketting, and is substantially thicker than the rest; 3in plank is used for this. Clamp is used under the deck beams of the upper deck, quarterdeck and forecastle. Obviously, it is thinner than that of the lower deck, so 3in seems suitable. The rest of the internal planking is 1½in thick, like that under the gundeck.

## THE PLANKING OF THE BOTTOM

According to John Smith, the bottom should be covered with 2in plank. The lowest plank, called the garboard strake, is shaped to fit into the rabbet of the keel. The upper planks should follow the lines of the wales. Planks should end at frames, and be bolted or treenailed to them. Towards the bows, it might be necessary to use short planks, known as 'stealers' to make up the necessary width. The planks of the *Sea Venture* seem to be 12in wide.

## THE UPPER EXTERNAL PLANKING

The planking up to the gunports is 2in thick. Above that, it should perhaps be narrowed to 1½in.

## BETWEEN THE WALES

The planking between the lower and the second wale was normally thicker than the other planking; therefore, it is 3in thick.

## THE WALES

The depth of the wales is given on pages 12–13. The thickness is taken from the survey of the *Moon*. The lower wale is given as 3in outside the plank. Since the plank is likely to be 3in thick at this point, the wale is 6in thick. Similarly, the second wale is 5in thick. The channel wales are 2in outside the plank, which is 1½in thick at that point. The gunwales and upper rails are the same thickness. The gunwale and the upper rails of the quarterdeck and forecastle are finished by a flat piece of timber extending inboard over the side of the ship. Externally, the depth of this is included in the depth of the gunwale.

## CHANNELS

The purpose of the channels is to spread the effect of the shrouds. Here, their thickness is half that of the channel wale, and visual sources suggest that this is approximately correct. The width of the channels is determined by the angle of the shrouds, all of them relatively narrow. But the fore channels are somewhat wider than the others, because they have to carry the shrouds clear of the forecastle. The widths of the channels are as follows:

| | |
|---|---|
| Fore | 1ft 9in |
| Main | 1ft 3in |
| Mizzen | 9in |

In each case, the deadeyes are placed 3in in from the edge of the channel. The fore and main channels have five shrouds each; the fore is 9ft 6in long, and the main is 12ft long. The mizzen channels have three shrouds each, and are 6ft long. The holes for the deadeyes are evenly spaced along the length, as there is no need to place them to avoid gunports. The first and last are about 6in in from the end of the channel. Because they are not very wide, there is probably no need to have them supported by wooden brackets.

## THE PLANKING OF THE DECKS

The plank of the lower deck is 2in thick (*Moon*). Presumably it should be in 12in wide strakes. Each plank should, of course, end at a deck beam, and be fixed to it. It is in parallel strakes, rather than 'swept'. Towards the bow and stern, the ends of the planks are butted into the waterways.

It is possible that the other decks should be constructed in the same way. On the other hand, there is some evidence that decks which bore no guns had a different sort of covering. The survey of the *Moon* indicates that the upper deck, quarterdeck and forecastle were covered with deal boards, 1½in thick, rather than planking. This system is shown on some old prints of ships.

## PILLARS

Instead of the crosspieces, which were evidently not used on such a small ship, vertical pillars are placed along the centreline, resting on the kelson, to give support to the middle of the decks. The middle part of the pillar is probably turned to give a decorative effect. As a rough guide, one is placed under every second beam.

## DECKS IN THE STORE ROOMS (C8, C9, C10)

Clearly there is no room in the bows and stern to give a full height of deck for either the bread room astern, or the store rooms forward, so there is only about 4ft headroom there. The forward platform is constructed with light deck beams, except that one has to bear the weight of the main bitts and is therefore made stronger. Ordinary decking, like that of the fore platform, is used, rather than gratings, as were used later. Possibly both are covered with deal rather than ordinary planking.

## METHODS OF FIXING

The main parts of the inner structure – frames, keel and kelson, deckhooks and transoms, etc, are held together by iron bolts, probably 1in in diameter. On the *Sea Venture*, the keel bolts are clenched over washers, while bolts in other places are either clenched or pinned.

The planks are fixed by treenails, with two driven though each plank where it meets a frame. The placing of them is rather random in relation to the individual frame, and it seems that this was deliberate, to help spread the load. Sometimes, the ends of the treenails were wedged, sometimes not.

# DECORATION

### THE LENGTH OF THE HEAD (D1)

The Admiralty Library manuscript suggests that the length of the head should be a fifth of the length of the keel, while Harriot suggests a fifth or a sixth: a fifth is used here. This length is measured from the fore edge of the stempost to the fore edge of the figurehead.

### CROSS-SECTION AND PLAN OF THE HEAD (D1, D2, D3)

Around 1600, there was a transition between two types of head. In the old type, the cross-section was quadrilateral with a flat bottom, and in the new type it had a V-shaped area added at its lower part. The old type has been used, as merchant ships tended to lag a little way behind the latest fashions.

In the plan view, the rails of the head have to run backwards from the figurehead until they form a tangent to the line of the timbers of the frame. This determines the main outline of the plan, and also determines how far the rails should run aft in the profile.

The head is supported by crosspieces, running across the knee of the head. It is planked, or covered with deals or gratings. The latter is perhaps the most likely, as it would allow any water shipped to drain away. This area was already in use for the crew's toilet facilities: there is no sign that any 'seats of ease' were erected at this time but, possibly, holes were cut to allow the human waste to fall out.

### THE PROFILE OF THE HEAD (D1)

There is no hard information on the height of the various parts of the head, but a study of the prints and drawings suggests that the upper rail is approximately at the height of the deck in the forecastle, and is a continuation of the upper channel wale. The lower rail is placed 2ft below that, at the after edge, and tapers towards the fore part.

The 'steeving', or angling upwards of the head, is given in the Admiralty Library manuscript as 120 or 130 degrees, though a footnote explains that this is impossible, and should read 12 or 13 degrees; 12 degrees has been used. This is measured on the lower rail, from end to end, without allowing for the curve in the middle.

The hancing piece, above the upper rail, is largely made up of a curve which takes it some way up the forecastle. According to the Admiralty Library manuscript, the radius of the circle should be 29/31 of the depth in hold, which makes it 8ft 11in.

The knee of the head fills the angle between the head and the stempost. In thickness it is a little less than the stempost itself.

### THE FIGUREHEAD (D4)

At this time the figurehead was still very small. It was placed at the fore end of the head, with its foot resting on the lower rail, and its head just protruding above the upper rail. This means that the figurehead of the *Susan Constant* is only about 2ft high. There is no hard information on figureheads of merchant ships of this period, but those of warships are either equestrian figures, or lions (see Photographs 2, 3). Neither of these seems appropriate for this ship, so a standing, fully-clothed female figure is used, to represent the name. Such a figure naturally has a vertical emphasis, whereas either a lion or a horse would have a more horizontal emphasis. Alternatively, the head could end in a scroll as in the Oxford model (see Photograph 4).

## THE STERN GALLERIES (D5, D6)

Stern and quarter galleries are drawn on the plan, largely because they were carried by the *Moon*, and she was an even smaller ship than the *Susan Constant*. At that period, old-fashioned stern galleries were entirely open, though some of the newest ships had small turrets added.

The Admiralty Library manuscript (p 29) suggests that the length of the galleries should be a sixth of the whole length. This can be taken to mean the length from the counter of the stern to the fore edge of the sternpost, and this is about 80ft on the *Susan Constant*. A sixth of this is 13ft. It is measured from the level of the stern timber, to give the length of the quarter gallery. The actual stern gallery extends aft of that, and aft of the stern itself.

The after end of the deck of the quarter gallery is placed at a level with the counter, as this seems to be indicated by the prints and drawings. The quarter galleries are angled downwards in relation to the line of the deck, so that, in this case, they are about a foot lower than deck level at the fore edge.

Clearly, the galleries have to be wide enough to allow a man to walk about with a reasonable degree of comfort, but at the same time not so wide that they create too much windage, or cause the appearance of the ship to become ridiculous. The stern gallery is a little wider than the quarter gallery. The sides of the gallery are 3½ft deep, as this seems a suitable minimum to protect men from being swept overboard.

The doors of the galleries cannot be placed in the extreme aftermost part of the stern, as the hull is very narrow at that point, and it leaves little room, especially if a door is fitted on each side. Furthermore, access would only be through the captain's quarters, and it is more likely that all the officers, and some of the higher-ranking passengers, would have the right to use the galleries. Therefore, they are placed some way forward, near the fore end of the galleries.

The galleries are supported by small brackets underneath the deck. The sides are framed by battens which are fitted directly above the brackets, and the sides are divided into approximately rectangular sections, for decorative effect. Other brackets are fitted under the stern gallery, on the same principle. It is possible that curved brackets could be placed above the galleries, extending from the top of the sides to the side of the hull. The sides of the galleries are covered with deal, and the deck is made in the same way. The sides of the galleries are vertical, but it is equally possible that they could be angled outwards, as this form sometimes appears in contemporary prints.

## CARVING

Wood carving was still rare on merchant ships at this time. It was just coming into use for the most prestigious warships, such as the *Prince* of 1610. The upper rails, above the level of the upper channel wale, would probably be formed in some kind of moulding. The knightheads, which support the bowsprit, were commonly carved, as the name suggests, with the head of a man, usually wearing a helmet. Likewise, the cathead got its name from the figure of a cat carved in its outer face. Perhaps there would be some carvings, probably in the form of figures, in a few other areas – the brackets of the head, the verticals of the bulkheads, for example. The style would be vernacular, as on the Swedish *Vasa*.

The wales and rails were evidently not decorated, except the gunwale. The rails of the *Vasa* are all square in cross-section, while those of the ship in the National Maritime Museum draught (Photograph 5) are all round. However, the upper gunwale is decorated.

## PAINTING

Most replicas of ships of this period rely heavily on the drawings in the Matthew Baker manuscript (Photograph 6), though it was twenty years old by this time. According to contemporary drawings, and a single model (see Photographs 4, 5, 7), the triangular style of decoration was being superseded in the latest warships, by a rather floriated style. Again, merchant ships would probably be a little behind warships in this respect, but less so in the case of painting than with carvings, so it is likely that the style of the Oxford model, the National Maritime Museum draught (Photograph 5) and the Danish draught (Photograph 7), would be appropriate for the *Susan Constant*.

In particular, the bow could be painted as in the Oxford model (Photograph 4), with the leaf-like painting on the main part, and with the twisted space below the hancing piece. The stern is divided into panels, and each of these could be painted in a different design, representing a particular theme – the signs of the zodiac (always important to mariners), or some other designs, perhaps copied from the Danish draught. Decoration along the whole length of the ship above the channels, as on the Danish draught, is not likely on a merchant ship.

An alternative colour scheme is to be found from Speed's map of Cornwall (Photograph 8). This shows a ship in brown and gold, with a much simpler design. It could be argued that it is more appropriate to a merchant ship of the period. In any case, the *Susan Constant* almost certainly had her decoration changed several times during her career, so it is impossible to reach any firm conclusion.

# FITTINGS

## THE RUDDER (E1)

There is no specific information on the fore and aft width of the rudder; it is, therefore, drawn so that it looks similar to that in contemporary prints. Its length should be enough to carry it up to the tuck, or the top of the sternpost, with some extra. The top part is curved to match the curve of the counter. It narrows quite sharply at the hancing, at the level of the load waterline. At its lower end, the rudder is the same width as the keel, and it widens as it rises, so that it is approximately square in cross-section at the uppermost part. The foremost edge of the rudder is rounded to allow it to turn against the sternpost.

## FITTING THE RUDDER (E2)

Mainwaring (p 214) mentions 4, 5 or 6 pintles for a rudder. Presumably, a small ship like the *Susan Constant* should have four. These are fitted to match the gudgeons on the sternpost. Both gudgeons and pintles are moulded in iron, with straps leading out, so that they can be bolted to the rudder and sternpost. The strap of the gudgeon should, of course, follow the local shape of the hull. The upper pintle was usually slightly longer than the others. Grooves were cut in the fore edge of the rudder to allow space for the pintle. To make fitting possible, the groove was longer than the pintle by the thickness of the gudgeon ring, plus a little extra. After fitting, the rudder was held in place by means of wedges.

## THE TILLER (A4)

The tiller has to be slightly curved, so that it can meet the rudder at an appropriate angle, and then meet the whipstaff just under the upper deck. In this respect, it is similar to the *Vasa*. At least one picture (see Photograph 9) shows a ship with the tiller fitted outside the head of the rudder, but the painting was by a Dutch artist, and it is more likely that he got it wrong, as this was typical Dutch style for fitting the tiller. Probably the tiller was fitted into a tenon in the rudder, in the common English fashion. The tiller starts off being square in section where it tenons into the rudder, and becomes rounded by the time it reaches the gooseneck of the tiller.

The end of the tiller is supported by a timber which is suspended from the deck beams above. This timber is probably quite short, as the movement of the tiller is rather limited in practice.

## THE WHIPSTAFF (E2, E3, E4, E5, E6)

All the written sources mention a whipstaff, and seem to imply that even small ships had it, though some state that the largest ships did not have one. It seems likely that one was fitted to the *Susan Constant*.

The whipstaff consists of two essential parts – the staff itself, which is vertical when the helm is centred, and which is held by the helmsman, and the 'rowle', which pivots at the level of the upper deck, with the staff passed through it. The lower end of the staff is attached to the end of the tiller by means of a metal 'gooseneck'. This system allows the whipstaff to be disengaged quickly when necessary, so that the ship can be steered by means of block and tackle in heavy weather.

In recent years, research has shown that there has been a basic misconception about the working of the whipstaff (see the article by Jean Boudriot in *Neptunia* (no 129, 1978, pp 56–62, *Nautical Research Journal* 1980, pp 149–54), also my book, *Fitting and Arming*, pp 15–16). Instead of being fixed to the rowle, the tiller was free to slide up and down inside it. This is partly confirmed by a statement by Mainwaring that 'when a ship doth draw down the helm and doth, as it were, suck the whipstaff out of his hand at the helm' (p 239). The actual movement given by the tiller was quite slight – about 15 degrees. In large changes of course, the ship was probably steered by the sails rather than the rudder.

When the sea was heavy, the whipstaff was removed from the tiller, and a block and tackle was fitted on each side, presumably just under the upper deck. According to Mainwaring (p 260), 'When the sea is so rough that men cannot govern the helm with their hands, then they seize two blocks to the helm on each side at the end, and reeving two falls through them like gunners tackles, bring them to the ships sides; so having some at one tackle, some at the other, they govern the helm as they are directed.'

## THE COMPASS AND BINNACLE (E7)

A ship like the *Susan Constant* would probably carry at least two compasses. The compass is gimballed within a box, and the whole assembly fits inside the binnacle like a drawer. The 'bittacle' is mentioned by Mainwaring and others, though there is little specific detail for that period. The nearest contemporary description is a French one of the 1660s – 'the bittacle . . . where there are three compartments, or sometimes four; in one is the light, in another is the compass . . . and in the third is the hour glass. If there is a fourth, a second compass is put in it.' (Fournier, quoted in *The Haven Finding Art*, (E G R Taylor, Hollis and Carter, 1971, p 234). It can be assumed that a small ship like the *Susan Constant* would have a simple compass in the binnacle, with at least one other kept aside as a spare and for taking bearings. In order to throw the light from the candle onto the compass and the hour glass at a suitable angle, the light is placed on one side, and the hour glass above the compass on the other. At night a sliding panel would be placed over the face of each side of the binnacle. The one on the candle side would be solid, while that on the other would have holes of minimum size to allow the helmsman to see the compass. The binnacle is fastened with wooden pins rather than iron nails, and is 'so contrived that they may carry a candle or lamp in them to give light to the compass, so as they disperse no light further, nor yet let any be seen about the ship' (Fournier, in *The Haven Finding Art*, p 99). Both Mainwaring and Smith seem to imply that only one compass was fitted in the binnacle; not two, as in later years. The binnacle should be placed before the whipstaff.

## NUMBER OF ANCHORS

Mainwaring (p 88) implies that a ship should have up to four main anchors, the sheet and the first, second and third bower anchors. The sheet is the largest of these, though it is not much bigger than the others. However, it is quite likely that a small ship like the *Susan Constant* would have only three main anchors, with only two bowers. A ship should also have a stream anchor and a kedge, much smaller than the others.

## SIZE OF ANCHORS

Mainwaring suggests that the proper proportion for a sheet anchor should be 1cwt for every 25t of the ship. This means the sheet anchor of the *Susan Constant* should be about 5cwt. The bowers should be slightly smaller – about 4cwt each, or a little more. A stream anchor should be about a third of the weight of the best bower –1 1/3cwt. A kedge anchor should be about half that – 2/3cwt.

# SHAPE AND SIZE OF ANCHORS

The shape and proportions of anchors changed very little over the centuries. Mainwaring gives some basic proportions, which still hold good two centuries later. The design of the *Susan Constant*'s anchors can, therefore, be based on Sutherland's drawing of more than a century later (see Photograph 10). The following table gives the detailed sizes of the *Susan Constant*'s anchors, based on the proportions given by Sutherland:

| | Sheet | Bowers | Stream | Kedge |
|---|---|---|---|---|
| Weight | 5cwt | 4¼cwt | 1⅓cwt | ⅔cwt |
| Cube root of weight | 1.71 | 1.62 | 1.1 | 0.87 |
| Length of the shank, mh | 7ft 9in | 7ft 4in | 5ft 0in | 3ft 11in |
| Size on the larger end of the shank, cd | 4.7in | 4.5in | 3in | 2.5in |
| Smaller end of shank, ef | 3.6in | 3.45in | 2.33in | 1.84in |
| Length of the square, gh | 14.7in | 13.9in | 9.45in | 7.48in |
| Length of the nut, gh[1] | 9.66in | 9.15in | 6.20in | 4.91in |
| Size of the nut, square, g | 0.97in | 0.91in | 0.62in | 0.49in |
| Internal diam of the ring, kl | 10.68in | 10.12in | 6.87in | 5.43in |
| Diam of the cross-section of the ring, 1, 2 | 1.68in | 1.60in | 1.08in | 0.86in |
| Diam of the hole for the ring, 1, 3 | 1.92in | 1.82in | 1.24in | 0.98in |
| Length of the crown, mb | 5.85in | 5.54in | 3.76in | 2.98in |
| Length of the arm | 2ft 10½in | 2ft 8¾in | 1ft 10¼in | 1ft 5½in |
| Breadth of the fluke, pq | 13.46in | 12.75in | 8.65in | 6.85in |
| Length of the fluke, R4 | 18.94in | 17.95in | 12.18in | 9.64in |
| Thickness of the fluke, 65 | 1.22in | 1.15in | 0.78in | 0.62in |
| Square at arm of fluke, R | 2.95in | 2.79in | 1.89in | 1.5in |
| Length of the bill, 4n | 4.40in | 4.17in | 2.83in | 2.24in |
| Rounding of the fluke, 2, 4[2] | 0.49in | 0.46in | 0.31in | 0.24in |
| Clutches of the arm, em | 17.66 | 16.73 | 11.36 | 8.99 |

[1] There are two 'g's marked on the diagram; the one referred to in this case is the lower of the two.
[2] Presumably this means the amount by which the rounded part of the fluke comes outside the straight line from 2 to 4.

Mainwaring also says that the beam, measured between the tips of the flukes, is two thirds of the length of the shank, this gives figures of:

| 5ft 2in | 4ft 10½in | 3ft 4in | 2ft 7⅓in |
|---|---|---|---|

The stock of the anchor is made of wood. It was probably made in two halves, held together by iron hoops, with a space between the halves so that the hoops could be driven further in if required.

## THE CATHEAD

The catheads were used to lift the anchors clear of the ship's sides when they were hoisted out of the water. One projected from each side of the forecastle. They were shown leading, directly forward, as this is shown in one of the Dutch prints of the Armada ships (Photograph 11), and this would be suitable for lifting the anchors; but it is also possible that they could project diagonally from the forecastle, as can be seen in Photograph 1.

There is no specific information on dimensions, but clearly a cathead should be strong enough to lift an anchor of 5cwt. It has two holes cut in its outer end to take the sheaves of the cat tackle. This consists of a double block with a hook, and a rope leading through that block and the sheaves of the cathead. When raising the anchor, the cat hook is put through the anchor ring (possibly by a seaman climbing onto the anchor stock), and then hoisted up to the cathead. The anchor is not kept attached to the cat block while the ship is under way, as it would be difficult to release in a hurry.

## THE STOWAGE OF THE ANCHORS

When not in use, the cat hook was taken out of the ring of the anchor, and the ring was supported by a 'stopper', a rope which passed through the ring and round the cathead; this allowed quick release. The other end of the anchor, the crown, was 'fished', which entailed placing a movable davit over the side, and lowering a tackle with a hook to catch the end of the anchor. The fish hook was much larger than the cat hook, as it had to hold the shank of the anchor, not merely the ring. The crown was raised until the shank was horizontal, the fish hook was taken off, and the crown held up by a stopper similar to that at the ring. When the ship was out of sight of land, the cable was removed from the anchor ring and taken inboard, and the hawse hole stuffed with a piece of wood, to keep seawater out.

The davit should have sheaves in it like the cathead. It should be long enough to be fixed in the middle of the forecastle, and to protect some way over the side – its length should probably equal the width of the forecastle. The 'spanshackle' is fitted in the middle of the deck of the forecastle. It is a large ringbolt, shaped to receive one end of the davit.

Only the bower anchors were stowed under the cathead. The sheet was probably lashed against the fore channels, like the stream and kedge.

## THE ANCHOR CABLES

According to Mainwaring (p 113), 'A cable is a three strand rope'. A manuscript in the British Library (Harl 253 f 65) suggests that a ship of 120 tons should have a cable 9in in circumference. Mainwaring suggests that 'they grow in greatness, beginning with the last until it come to the sheet anchor cable'. According to a formula of 1642, the sheet cable should be 1/24 of the main beam, though, in practice, most ships seem to have used less than this (see *Arming and Fitting* p 44). The formula would give 11in for the *Susan Constant*; so 10in for the sheet cable, and 9in for the bower cables, seems a suitable compromise. A ship invariably had more cables than anchors, and a total of six cables, exclusive of kedge and stream cables, seems right. A cable was normally 120 fathoms long.

On larger ships, the cables were stowed on the orlop deck, but of course this is impossible on the *Susan Constant*. In the 1800s, British sixth-rate warships stowed their cables in the hold, on top of the barrels. There is no proof that this was used earlier, but it seems likely. Some could be put on top of the upper tier but, if necessary, gaps could be left in the upper tier to allow space, with the cables stowed on the second tier. The cables are passed through the main hatch when the anchor is being raised or lowered.

There should be numerous smaller cables and 'cablets', for the smaller anchors, and for towing, etc.

## THE HAWSE HOLES (E10)
The cables pass through hawse holes, cut in the bows of the ship near the stem. They are as high as possible in the bows, which means just under the lower rail of the head. Four were probably used, two on each side of the stem. In the seventeenth century it seems to have been normal to have the inner one on each side a little lower than the outer one. The hawse hole had a diameter at least twice that of the cable. Since the largest cable on the *Susan Constant* has a diameter of a little over 3in, this indicates that the diameter of the hawse holes would be about 7½in.

There is no evidence that the hawse holes of this period were reinforced with bolsters, or enclosed within the 'cheeks of the head', as was to happen in later years.

## THE BITTS (A4)
The bitts were strong timber structures intended to take the strain while the ship was riding at anchor. The bitt pins were stout vertical pieces of timber, reaching downwards into the hold where they were fixed to the timbers of the hull, or to riders. Both Mainwaring and Smith suggest that only one pair of pins was fitted at this time. They were placed side by side, and forward of the foremast, where there is room for them, and they do not interfere with the guns. They protrude some way above the lower deck, as that is where the cables are handled. The crosspiece of the bitts passes between the two pins, and is recessed slightly into them. It protrudes some way outside the pins, so that the cable can be looped round an end of the crosspiece and the head of one of the pins, in figure-of-eight fashion, to give greater holding power. A large knee is placed forward of each bitt pin, fixed to the deck beams, serving to brace the pin against the pull on the anchor cable.

## THE MANGER (A4)
The manger is a light structure right forward on the lower deck, intended to retain most of the water which will come in through the hawse holes when the ship is anchored in heavy seas. Mainwaring suggests it should be 18in high. It is constructed of vertical battens, with light planks slotted into them. In this case, it is built round the bitts.

## THE CAPSTAN (E8, E9)
The ship is fitted with one double capstan, placed forward of the mainmast. Some accounts suggest that it should be aft of the mainmast, but there is rather less room for it there. Many ships would have had a single capstan in that position, operating only on the upper deck; but that would only serve for lifting weights on deck, as there would be nothing to work the anchor cables on the lower deck. It is not likely that the *Susan Constant* is big enough to merit two capstans.

On the 'drumhead' capstan, each bar is fitted into a recess on an enlarged head; none of the bars passed all the way through the head, and all the bars were kept on the same level. This type does not appear until the 1670s, and so the older type is used. Each bar passes right through the capstan, so that they all have to be on different levels. Only two bars are needed on such a small ship.

The barrel forms the central part of the capstan. It is made from a single piece of timber, cut to a twelve-sided cross-section. The lowest part is circular, and much smaller, to rotate in a hole cut in the lower deck partners. The 'whelps' serve to increase the diameter for hauling in the rope, and to increase friction with the rope. They are shaped to prevent the rope from riding up too far. They are tenoned into the spindle on each alternate face, and reinforced by chocks, which are tenoned into the whelps. There are two sets of whelps: one at upper deck level, used for lifting spars, guns, cargo, etc, and another at lower deck level, used for hauling the anchor. However, the bars are fitted only at upper deck level; this was normal until about the 1720s. The pauls are fitted to the decks; they come in pairs, one to operate in each direction, and are made of iron, about an iron pivot, they were intended to prevent the capstan surging backwards. Presumably, there should be a pair on each deck.

The design of the capstan is largely based on one recovered from a Swedish warship of 1600, in Stockholm, with references to *Deane's Doctrine* to confirm that English practices were not different.

## THE VIOL (E10)
On large ships, the cable itself was not coiled round the capstan. Instead, the viol was led to it. Smith seems to imply that this system was also used on small ships in case of difficulty. The viol should have a circumference about 60 per cent of the largest cable, which means 6in. It is an 'endless' rope, in that the two ends are eye-spliced and then lashed together.

## DRAINAGE IN THE BILGES
Holes, known as 'limber holes', are drilled in the floor timbers, with a line of them running fore and aft. These allowed the bilge water which finds its way between the frames to drain towards midships, at the lowest point of the hold. In order to clean these holes out periodically, a rope runs through the whole line; it is, presumably, considerably smaller in diameter than the holes themselves. This is pulled back and forward occasionally to help clean the holes of gravel ballast, etc.

## THE SITUATION OF THE PUMPS (A4)
Obviously, the pumps have to be placed close to the lowest part of the bilges, which, in practice, means close to the mainmast. Small ships usually had two pumps, and this is confirmed by the survey of the *Moon*. They are, therefore, placed just forward of the mainmast, with one on each side, just within the area of the mainmast partner. They are angled inwards, so that their lower ends are close to the kelson. The lower end is below the ceiling, so that the intake is between the frames of the hull. They have to operate at the level of the lower deck, so that the water is brought above the waterline and can be allowed to drain overboard. Below the lower deck, the pump is enclosed in light boards, to form the 'well'. This keeps the cargo and ballast from getting in the way of the pump, and allows a certain amount of access for maintenance.

## THE CONSTRUCTION OF THE PUMPS (E11, E12)
The pumps of the *Moon* were brake pumps, and this was normal on small ships. This means that they were suction pumps rather than chain pumps, operated by means of a lever, or 'brake'. They were also known as 'elm tree pumps', indicating that the tube of the pump was a piece of elm that had been bored out. The exterior of the tube was tapered from top to bottom. The brake

was pivoted on an arm extending diagonally from the head of the tube. It was linked to a 'spear', which led down inside the tube. The spear was connected to the upper box, which moved up and down inside the tube, with the movement of the brake. The box was fitted with a non-return valve made of leather, which opened on the downward stroke to allow the water to pass through. There was another box, which was fixed in position near the bottom of the tube. At the upper end of the pump, the water would leave by means of a small pipe near the head. It is possible that this could be connected to another pipe, known as a 'dale', which would lead the water to the side of the ship. There was no cistern to retain the water after it left the tube.

There does not seem to have been much change in brake pumps in the century and a half after the *Susan Constant*, and those of the *Vasa* are quite similar to those in British ships much later. The drawings are based on those of the *Vasa*, on drawings of British ships of the eighteenth century, and on parts recovered from the *Invincible* of 1744.

## THE SCUPPERS (E13, E14)
Scuppers were lead pipes fitted in holes cut through the waterways and the side planking of the ship. They allowed water, including that pumped from the bilges, to drain over the side. A flat plate was moulded on the inboard end, to help with fixing the scupper. A leather flap was hung on the hole on the outside, to prevent seawater from entering the hull.

There is one scupper for each side in the manger, forward on the lower deck. In addition, the gunroom, the steerage, the rise of the upper deck and the rise of the lower deck each have one on each side. The main parts of the upper and the lower decks have two each side, with one on the lower deck close to the pumps.

## THE NUMBER AND TYPES OF BOATS
Every ship of any size carried a longboat, and, to judge from the surveys of the navy of the 1620s, a ship of about 120 tons should carry one other boat (though we cannot rule out the possibility that a ship on such a long voyage would carry more, with a view to leaving some behind for the use of the colonists). There is no doubt that the *Susan Constant* also carried a shallop – Smith mentions that 'our' shallop was 'built up' soon after landing in Virginia. It is not clear whether this means that her sides were built up higher for defence, or whether it was carried in pieces in the hold of the ship, and constructed after arrival. The latter seems more likely, as she was launched after being built, and this would not have been an event worthy of notice unless the boat was new built. Furthermore, the use of the term 'our' might be taken to mean that the boat belonged to the colonists rather than the ship. Both Smith and Mainwaring agree that the second boat carried by a ship should be a 'skiff or shallop'.

As a type, the longboat remained in use for more than a century and a half after the *Susan Constant*, and it is not too difficult to know what kind of boat is meant. It was large, heavy, broad, and was usually fitted with a windlass and a stern davit for anchor work. The shallop is much more obscure, largely because it disappeared from naval service soon after 1618, on the recommendation of a Commission of Enquiry. In the surveys of the 1620s, virtually every ship had a longboat, but only one, the *Prince Royal*, had a shallop. Several more were in store, presumably because they had been withdrawn from use, but their dimensions are not given. The *Moon* was to be issued with a 20ft longboat, and this seems approximately right for the *Susan Constant*. She also had a 14ft jollyboat. This length is used for her second boat, but it should be a shallop instead of a jollyboat.

## THE DESIGN OF THE LONGBOAT (E15)
The basic dimensions of the longboat of the *George*, surveyed in 1626, were:

| | |
|---|---|
| Length | 21ft 3in |
| Breadth | 7ft 5in |
| Depth | 2ft 8in |

These dimensions are used for the longboat of the *Susan Constant*, as it would be risky to try to scale them down to find the dimensions of the *Moon*'s boat.

There are no scale drawings of English boats of this period, or any time before 1700. However, there are very detailed dimensions and specifications for boats from the 1680s onwards, and these are enough to provide a reconstruction. The scantlings of longboats can be found from a document of 1690 (*Arming and Fitting* p 295) but, for the dimensions of the sweeps, rising lines, etc, it is necessary to use the dimensions of 1719.

## THE DESIGN OF THE SHALLOP (E16)
There is some information on jollyboats of 1625 and later, but virtually nothing on shallops, except for the dimensions of that carried by the *Prince Royal* (27ft × 6ft 9in × 2ft 4in). It might be possible to scale this down to give proportional dimensions for a 14ft boat, giving a breadth of 3ft 9in, and a depth of 1ft 2½in. However, there is no evidence of a boat with such small length and breadth, then or later; presumably, it would have been unseaworthy. The smallest breadth and depth are those given for the jollyboat of the *Moon*, and, therefore, these dimensions are used, since it is evident that the difference between a jollyboat and a shallop was not necessarily to be found in the proportions of length to breadth to depth.

According to Mainwaring (p 103), 'Other smaller boats which they carry for lightness to hoist in or out quickly are called shallops according to their form.' Smith (p 33) refers to 'small boats called shallops and skiffs, which are with more ease and less trouble rowed to and again upon any small occasion.' This does not tell us a great deal. Several prints of colonial expeditions of the time show small boats in use, with rounded sterns instead of transoms; perhaps this illustrates the essential feature of the shallop, which differentiates it from other boats. On this assumption, the shallop for the *Susan Constant* is designed using the dimensions of the jollyboat of the *Moon*, and the details of a jollyboat of 1680 (*Arming and Fitting* pp 294–5), but with a round stern. The smallest of the jollyboats described there has dimensions of:

| | |
|---|---|
| Length (excluding stem and stern) | 13ft 3in |
| Total length | approximately 17ft |
| Breadth | 5ft 2in |
| Depth | 2ft 2in |

This is slightly different from the proportions of 1626. The dimensions have been scaled to those in the appropriate plane, of length, breadth and depth, except where it is necessary to make alterations to round off the stern, but this method is unsatisfactory. It is quite possible that the ship should not have a shallop at all, except one carried in pieces in the hold.

## STOWAGE OF THE BOATS
Most sources agree that a longboat of this period was not hoisted in, but was towed behind, even when the ship was at sea. It was hauled by two ropes, the boat rope and the gust rope. A shallop, on the other hand, would be hoisted aboard using tackle attached to the main stay and the fore and mainyards. It would probably be stowed on the upper deck, and there is room for it on the starboard side, aft of the mainmast, where it would not interfere with anything else.

## SHEATHING OF THE HULL

Ships on voyages to the West Indies were normally sheathed, and this probably applied to the *Susan Constant*. The hull below the waterline was covered with a mixture of hair and tar, and then planked over. The planking used at that time was normally ½in thick, and elm was the most common wood used, being softer than oak. The sheathing was then payed over with 'white stuff' – a mixture of train oil, rosin and brimstone, giving a white finish.

# ACCOMMODATION

### NUMBER OF PEOPLE ON BOARD

According to Purchas, there were 71 people on board the *Susan Constant* during the voyage. This would appear to be exclusive of the crew. Davis (p 59) says that ships in the Virginia trade carried one man for every 9.8 tons in 1686. He believes that slightly more would have been carried earlier in the century, and this seems likely in view of the difficult nature of the *Susan Constant*'s voyage. Using this figure gives twelve men for the ship; this should be increased to about fourteen. Room has, therefore, to be found for beds for 85 men, of varying quality and comfort according to the status of their occupants. Some would have had cabins to themselves, others would have shared them, while the common seamen and the artisans among the colonists would merely have a portion of deck.

### BEDS OR HAMMOCKS?

The hammock was certainly coming into use by the time of the Virginia voyage. In 1597, the navy had ordered canvas to make 'hanging cabins or beds', and this quite possibly means hammocks. They were being issued to ships in 1629, for overseas service only, and on a scale of one for two men. Clearly they were far from universal, and there is no certainty that they would have been used on a ship like the *Susan Constant*. The alternative would be straw palliasses laid out on deck, while men of middling rank would perhaps have a small wooden bed to enclose the palliasse. As late as the 1630s, Boteler mentions 'those wainscot beds wherein men use to sleep, being fastened to the ship's sides' (p 20).

The *Susan Constant* was overcrowded, even by the standards of the time, when two tons per passenger seems to have been regarded as normal. In Drake's expedition of 1596 'Brazil beds' or hammocks were supplied for the ships – though only 927, for a total number of about 2500 seamen and soldiers. This suggests that the hammock was used mainly to supplement other bedding on crowded ships. It is just possible to provide single and double cabins for all the gentlemen, and to find enough remaining space on the decks for mattresses for the other colonists. But it seems likely that Christopher Newport, a man experienced in America and West Indian voyages, would be familiar with the hammock, and would have acquired a few for his ships.

### THE COMPOSITION OF THE CREW

A ship of 120 tons would probably need a captain and two mates as 'executive' officers. All ships would also have a gunner, boatswain and carpenter, a cook, and perhaps a purser. Each of these would be entitled to a single cabin. There would be three or four petty officers, including perhaps a quartermaster, a boatswain's mate and a steward. These would probably have no special privileges with respect to accommodation. This would leave only five common seamen, so, clearly, the officers would often have to help with the manual labour.

### THE NUMBER OF CABINS (F1, F2)

Cabins were quite common at this time, even for ordinary sailors; this is perfectly clear from reading Smith, Mainwaring and Boteler, (see *Arming and Fitting* p 155). Most of them would have been very small, and probably held two men. 'But care should be had that there be not two comrades upon one watch, because they have the more room in their cabins to rest' (Smith p 49).

Possibly this means that the seamen shared small double beds, like the one found on the *Vasa*. Clearly the 'gentlemen' among the colonists would not have accepted worse conditions than the ordinary seamen, and would probably have demanded parity with the officers. One way round this would have been to put the seamen out of their cabins and give them to some of the colonists; another would be to build extra cabins so that all the space between decks was taken up with them. To consider the practicalities of this, it is necessary to measure out the space below deck, and attempt to allocate it.

## THE ALLOCATION OF SPACE (F2, F3)

Some areas can be assigned without too much difficulty. The area under the quarterdeck was reserved for the 'executive' officers, and will be discussed later. The gunroom was given to the gunner, but this seems too much space for one man in a crowded ship, so it can be divided into cabins, most of which can be given to the highest ranking colonists. There is room for six cabins, one for the gunner and five for the colonists. The space under the forecastle contains the cook room, with perhaps a cabin for the cook, and room for 'ready use provisions', but it still leaves enough room for the bulk of the crew. This leaves the central and forward parts of the lower deck. Space has so far been found for six of the crew, and five colonists. We still have to find room for nine crewmen, and 66 colonists.

John Smith suggests that mates, gunner and carpenter would be aft of the mast, and accommodated under the quarterdeck, or in the gunroom. He also says that 'the boatswain and all the younkers or common sailors under his command is to be before the mast' (p 49). This probably means in the forecastle, for if the ship was fully loaded with cargo on a normal voyage, she would presumably have her lower deck filled with lighter goods, allowing only enough space to work the guns. It is just possible to fit a cook room and nine members of the crew under the forecastle. The cook has been given a single cabin, opening directly into the cook room, and the latter is accessible by only one entrance, for security reasons. The boatswain is given a single cabin on the opposite side, slightly larger in accordance with his status. There is room for two more cabins, one on each side of the deck, for two crewmen each. These could share double beds. The remaining three crewmen sleep on straw mattresses on the deck.

We are now left with the gundeck, forward of the gunroom bulkhead, to accommodate 66 colonists. First, it is necessary to attempt to calculate the ranks of the colonists. According to Smith, 105 men stayed behind to found the colony, and of these 36 were councillors or gentlemen, the rest artisans, labourers, etc. Assuming that the gentlemen abandoned the voyage, or died on the way across, in the same proportions as the others, and that they were distributed evenly throughout the fleet, we find that about 24 gentlemen would have been aboard the *Susan Constant*. Five have already been given cabins in the gunroom, leaving nineteen in the forward part of the deck. Allowing space for the guns, there is just room for two double and two single cabins in the fore peak, accommodating six of the men. Six cabins can be located along the sides of the central part of the lower deck, leaving plenty of space for the guns, which would accommodate twelve men, and the remaining gentleman can be accommodated by making one of the single cabins in the gunroom into a double one. This leaves quite a large clear area forward on the gundeck, which can be used as messes for the artisans and labourers.

This leaves 47 colonists of lower rank to sleep on the deck or in hammocks, which seems possible – especially if some of them sleep in hammocks. In placing them, it is necessary to follow certain rules: room has to be left for the guns, capstans, pumps, masts, etc; a continuous corridor has been left down each side, to allow movement; the ladders have, of course, to be kept clear. Giving each man a space of 5ft 6in × 18in, it is possible to find room for about 34 men on the deck itself, with thirteen more in hammocks. Alternatively, some of the men could sleep on the floor in the gunroom and forepeak – probably, the servants of the leading colonists. Despite the hardships, the lower-ranking colonists actually have more room than the seaman of Nelson's time, who had only 14in to sling his hammock.

## OFFICERS' CABINS ON THE UPPER DECK (F4)

By long tradition, the captain and mates lived in the stern, on the upper deck (not on the quarterdeck at this period, even in ships which had a poop). The captain would have the use of the 'great cabin', in the aftermost part of the deck. Forward of that, there is room for three cabins on each side, with almost 6ft length in each. It is assumed that all the inhabitants of the upper deck would have the right to use the stern galleries for recreation, so this raises the question of access: unless they went through someone else's cabin, one of the doors had to be left clear. Therefore, a space is left on one side of the deck. This also adds to the size of the central area, which could serve as a dining room for the officers and the most senior of the colonists. Of the five cabins that are left, the aftermost one can be given to the captain, allowing him private access to the stern gallery. It would be neater to use this as his sleeping cabin, but a bed in such a confined space would block all access to the door, so the captain has to sleep in the great cabin and use the other one for dining and recreation. Two more cabins are used by the two mates, and another one, on the starboard side, is used as a chart room. The last cabin in this area is given to the carpenter, who, according to Smith, should be abaft the mast. Perhaps the chart room could be used as a cabin. This would allow one of the senior colonists to move into it, and ease the pressure on the lower deck. However, the ship's officers would be very jealous of their privileges, and social pressures would tend to keep them separate from the gentlemen.

## TYPES OF BEDS

The simplest type of bed is the palliasse or straw mattress. These could be either single or double, but single ones allow more flexibility in the berthing arrangements, so they seem most likely for the artisans and labourers among the colonists, and for the seamen who are not in cabins. A length of 5ft 6in is assumed, and a width of about 18in. When not in use, they could be stowed in some convenient place on deck. Such beds are mentioned in several documents. Lindsey's fleet orders of 1635 demand that 'no bed of straw, or combustible matter, be aboard in time of fight' (Monson IV p 9) – implying that they were to be thrown overboard, or perhaps stowed in the hold. Conversely, in an expedition of 1626 it was ordered that 'all beds and sacks in every ship should be disposed and used for the defence against the shot of the enemy' (*Medicine and the Navy* p 163). As early as 1557, it was suggested that hammocks were a healthy alternative to 'beds of grass' (J J Keevil, *Medicine and the Navy* vol 1, F & S Livingstone, Edinburgh, 1957, p 115).

The seamen in cabins could be given small double beds, with a length of 5ft 6in, and a breadth of 28in. This corresponds to the fourteen inches for a man, allowed in later years; it also tends to add significance to Smith's remark that if the two men are in a different watch 'they may have more room in their cabins to rest' (p 49). The mattress for such a bed would be placed inside a small wainscot box, which is lashed to the side. Something similar was discovered aboard the *Vasa* (see Margaret Rule, *The Mary Rose*, p 121).

Presumably, the gentlemen colonists who had to share cabins would demand something better than this, especially as they did not stand watches, and would all be asleep at the same time. There is just enough room in each cabin for two single beds, 5ft 6in by 18in. Presumably, one could be stacked on top of another in the daytime.

The ship's officers and the senior colonists would, of course, have beds in single cabins. It is quite possible that they would have provided their own mattresses, filled with something more comfortable than straw. There is room for a bed about 2ft wide in each of the cabins. Possibly, there would be some division of status within the group, with the captain and the most senior gentlemen having better beds than the common ones. The later type of officers' bed was raised some way above the deck with drawers underneath.

## THE CONSTRUCTION OF CABINS (F5, F6)
Surveys of naval ships of the period mention two basic types of cabin – 'boarded' and 'hanging' (see *Trinity House Transactions* p 91, for example). The boarded cabin is a more or less permanent construction, made of deal board framed with wooden battens; cabins can only be made like this when they do not get in the way of the running of the ship, operation of the guns, etc. Furthermore, they are likely to be the cabins which are used for any voyage, and not just set up temporarily when large numbers of passengers are on board. This means, in effect, that all the crew cabins, under the quarterdeck and under the forecastle, could be boarded cabins.

It is also possible that some of the cabins on the lower deck could be boarded. The two aftermost in the gunroom are some distance from the guns. On the other hand, they would have to be removable if gunports were fitted in the stern. Likewise, all the cabins in the central part of the deck are reasonably clear of guns; but they would have been fitted for this one voyage only, and are more likely to have been hanging cabins. All the cabins in the fore peak are close to the guns, and would get in the way if they were left up during anchor work, so they will certainly be removable.

It is quite clear that hanging cabins were made of canvas. This could mean that they were formed simply by canvas hanging like a curtain, suspended from hooks in the upper deck beams and perhaps laced to hooks on the lower deck. Alternatively, they could be slightly more complex structures, with the canvas stretched over wooden frames. This is suggested by a reference in 1628 to 'hanging cabins to fold up to the decks as lodging for the men' (*Trinity House Transactions* p 91) the editor takes this to mean hammocks (mistakenly in my opinion). Presumably, the hanging cabins would still be suspended from the deck above, to retain the name of 'hanging cabins'. They would have some kind of door, made in the same way for lightness. When they were folded away in action, the upper edge would perhaps remain suspended from the deckhead, while the lower edge would be lifted up and hung from the deck.

## MESSING ARRANGEMENTS (F7)
Smith says that a seamen's mess consists of four men, but he does not say whether they ate at tables or not. However Boteler says that one of the duties of a joiner is to 'settle the tables and fix them' (p 20). On the assumption that the seamen had tables, and that all the colonists would have expected the same, it becomes necessary to find space for the tables, and for the seats which would go with them.

Clearly, there is enough room under the quarterdeck for a table to seat about five men – the captain, two mates, gunner and carpenter. The gunroom has room for two tables, for twelve of the twenty-four gentlemen. Two more tables

can be put in the after part of the gundeck proper, for the remaining gentlemen, six at each table. The table for the seamen would be in the forecastle, in the space just aft of the foremast. The remaining 47 colonists would have tables arranged in the forward part of the gundeck proper – perhaps six would be needed, with eight men to each. Giving each man a 2ft space, and one at each end, would make each table 6ft × 2ft 6in, or so.

Tables suspended from the deck above are rather unlikely – they would be very unstable unless they had firm fixing to the side of the ship, and this is impossible with the cabins arranged as they are. If folding tables were in use at that time, they would provide one solution. Alternatively, the tables could be stacked in odd corners at night – under the ladders, and above the main hatch, where men would not sleep. The cabins for the crew and for the gentlemen could probably be kept in place all the time.

Bench-type seats would be provided for the common seaman and the artisans, perhaps with an upturned half-barrel as an extra seat at each end; the officers and gentlemen would have individual seats, perhaps with comfort and decoration according to status.

## THE FURNITURE OF CABINS
Obviously, the officers of the ship would expect to be on board for some considerable time, and would do their best to make their cabins comfortable, bringing their own furniture on board – tables, chairs, sea chests, etc. Each seaman would probably have room for a single sea chest, which could also serve as a seat when necessary. The passengers would not be able to carry much furniture, especially since they could not expect to return home with the ship. Movable furniture was presumably left to individual choice, so there would be no uniformity. There was probably some fixed furniture as well. Boteler's joiner is expected 'to contrive handsome and convenient benches in the cabins and round house and elsewhere for the stowing of small commodities; to make also those little boxes by the ships sides which are called lockers' (p 20). However, Mainwaring (p 181) implies that lockers were only used for storing shot, not for personal belongings, as in later years.

## PERSONAL BELONGINGS
Accepting Mainwaring's implication that lockers were not used for personal belongings, it can be assumed that seamen kept theirs in sea chests, while the passengers may also have had boxes or bags for changes of clothes, etc. But most of the passengers belongings would probably be stored in the hold.

## THE COOK ROOM (F8, F9, F10)
The term 'galley' was not yet in use to describe the ship's cook room. The location is in the forecastle – Smith, Mainwaring and others recommend that warships should have the cook room in the hold, but imply that merchant ships would have it in the forecastle, so that the cargo would not be disturbed. In construction, it consists simply of an iron bar, running fore and aft to hold a cooking pot, and an area built of fire bricks to contain the fire. There is no chimney: the smoke is allowed out by means of gratings placed above the brickwork. Such a cook room has been found in the hold of the *Vasa*. Similar ones were fitted on English warships of the time, as is shown by the surveys of the 1620s. As usual, the details are taken from the survey of the *Moon*. This gives a kettle of 2ft breadth, 17in deep; another 1ft broad, 7in deep; and a pease pot with cover, 8in broad, 15in deep. It is assumed that the kettles were circular – like all those recovered from wrecks of that century – and that

breadth means, in fact, diameter. It can be assumed that all the kettles were made of copper, but whether there was a lid is not clear.

The size of the brick furnace is determined by the size of the kettle – it has to be slightly larger, to allow room for the kettle to swing with the movement of the ship. The standard English brick of the period was 9in by 4½in by 2¼in (Alec Clifton Taylor, *The Pattern of English Building*, Faber & Faber, 1972, p 249). The furnace has to be placed in the centre of the ship, in order that the grating above will also be central. The cook room is built round it. Two sides of the brickwork can be built right up to the deck above, in order to protect the partition from fire. The other two are kept relatively low, so that the cook can get in to tend the fire. A double door is placed in the bulkhead of the forecastle, large enough to allow one of the butts to be brought in with ready-use supplies. The whole assembly has to be reasonably secure from theft, so this is the only full entrance. However, there may have been a small hatch to the crew's quarters forward, fitted with sliding doors, to avoid having to walk round with food.

Besides the kettle, there would have been other cooking equipment, such as a grill and a spit for turning. The survey of the *Mary Rose*, taken in 1626, gives some indication of what might be used:

> 1 bar of iron cross the cook room
> 1 hook to hang the kettle upon
> 1 pair of andirons
> 1 pair of tongs
> 1 fire shovel
> 1 spit
> 1 flesh hook
> 1 fire fork
> 3 gamming hooks
> 4 esses
> 1 iron to lay before the fire
> 2 furnaces of copper
> 1 fish kettle of copper
> 1 small kettle of copper

## SANITARY ARRANGEMENTS

The head was already in use as the main toilet accommodation. There is no evidence that seats were constructed as in later years, but presumably round holes were left in the deck. Another seventeenth-century feature was the 'piss-dale'. This was a kind of urinal, made of lead, shaped rather like a basin, and fitted to the side in the waist, with a pipe leading out through the side. There is no specific evidence that the piss-dale was in use so early in the century. Otherwise, the men presumably used chamber pots in their cabins and about the decks. Men of this period had little concept of privacy.

## THE STOWAGE OF THE HOLD (F11)

The ballast was placed at the lowest level in the hold. There would perhaps be a layer of pig-iron, and certainly a thicker layer of gravel. This would serve to level off the floor of the hold, to make stowage easier and provide a base for other stores.

Most of the goods in the hold would be food and water, especially the former. Such goods were kept in wooden casks, mostly butts. According to information in the *Trinity House Transactions*, the standard butt of the time was 2ft 8in in diameter, which means it must have been 4ft long. Three layers, or 'tiers' of butts were considered normal. Smaller casks, such as puncheons and hogsheads, would be used to fill up the awkward spaces near the sides. Other goods, such as the parts of the pinnace, and personal belongings, would probably be stored on top of the casks.

## BULKHEADS (F12, F13, F14)

The main bulkheads, at the forward end of the quarterdeck and after end of the poop, had to be quite strong, as they were intended as last refuge for the crew if the ship was boarded. This concept was becoming a little outdated by this time, and it is possible that only a pretence was kept up. However, the bulkheads would be constructed of fairly stout timber, perhaps 2in-thick planking. This is continued all the way down to the lower deck, as the parts below were also considered 'defensible'. The forward bulkhead of the forecastle would also be quite strong, as it was in a very exposed position. It is unlikely that the planks would be overlapped, as in Dutch ships, but would probably be carvel laid.

The doors in the bulkheads are largely determined by other factors. The double door to the cook room, and the single door to the seamen's quarters, dominate the forecastle bulkhead. The bulkhead below needs a central double door, carefully placed to allow a free run to the cables as they come in towards the capstan. Probably, only one of these doors would be needed for everyday use, and a small ladder is placed aft of that one. A small hole is left at the bottom of each door, so that when the ship is at anchor the cables can be led back to the hold from the bitts. The bulkhead of the quarterdeck needs an access door on one side, and a central window so that the man at the whipstaff can see the sails. Probably, this would be left open in good weather. It is not certain whether glass would actually have been used in this position. The bulkhead of the gunroom is subject to less constraint, and a simple door to one side is all that is needed, for access. Probably, all the bulkheads should have loopholes for muskets. The forward bulkhead needs only one door, to give access to the beakhead and the bowsprit.

The bulkheads of the bread room and store rooms are rather lighter. They have no doors, as access is through hatches in the deck above.

## HATCHES AND LADDERS (F15)

There is a main hatch in both the upper and lower deck, one directly above the other. This serves for access to the hold, and must be big enough to take a butt. Possibly there should be a smaller hatch in the after part of the hold, as that area is rather difficult to get to through the main hatch. There are smaller hatches, known as 'scuttles', to the bread room aft and the store rooms forward. These should have some form of locking, to prevent theft. Gratings are also placed on the weather decks, to give light and air to the decks below. The 'steam gratings' are placed directly above the furnace in the cook room, to allow smoke to escape, as there was no chimney.

Short ladders give access to the falls of the gundeck and upper deck. There are two ladders to give access from the upper deck to the lower, and these are the main means of communication. These two are placed centrally, as are all the hatches and scuttles in the deck, for reasons of safety. The forecastle and quarterdeck are reached by one ladder each, offset to one side to allow the placing of doors. Another ladder leads down from the forecastle to the foredeck, so that access to the beakhead need not be through the seamen's quarters.

All the major holes in the deck, for hatches, gratings, ladders, etc, are surrounded by a coaming, a low wall of wood, about 6in high. All, including the ladderways, could be closed in bad weather, so a recess was cut to allow a wooden cover to be fitted when needed. In the case of the hatches, these usually held the gratings, or solid wood covering in the case of the scuttles.

The gratings were constructed of ledges running athwartships, and battens running fore and aft. The ledges were about 3in square in cross-section, and were recessed to take the battens; these were 3in wide, but only about ¾in deep, except for the outermost ones, which were as deep as the ledges. The battens and ledges were about 3in apart, with slight variations according to the actual size of the grating.

# MASTS AND YARDS

### TYPES AND SIZES OF MASTS (G1, G2, G3)

The siting of the lower masts has already been discussed (p 11). A ship of this size should have three masts plus a bowsprit. The spritsail topsail does not seem to have been carried by ships as small as this, but the fore and the main should have topmasts.

The lengths are also taken from Anderson. He suggests, from the study of various sources, that the mainmast of a large ship should be 2½ times the beam, while that of a small ship should be up to three times. Since the *Susan Constant* is near the smaller end of the scale, a figure of about 2.8 is used. (Note that the mast is measured from the heel, where it joins the step in the hold, to the head, above the overlap between it and the topmast.) This gives a length of 63ft 3in.

According to Anderson, the head of the foremast should be approximately level with the trestletrees on the main; so, first it is necessary to find the position of the trestletrees. By about 1600, these should be about 1/15 of the way down from the head of the main, giving 4ft 2½in. This makes the foremast 53ft 11in long, or 0.85 of the length of the mainmast. Mainwaring suggests 0.8 for this, while slightly later sources suggest 0.8888, so 0.85 is not unreasonable. The length of the foremast above the trestletrees is 4/5 of that of the main mast – 3ft 5in. The head of the mizzen should be about halfway up the fore masthead.

The mizzen, unlike the other masts, was not stepped on the keel. Clearly, it would have been impossible to fit a long enough tiller if the mizzen went any way below the upper deck. This is where the mast was stepped on the *Vasa*. The length of the mizzen is 40ft 5in.

Anderson suggests that a main topmast of this period should be a little more than half the length of the mainmast, which gives 33ft. The fore topmast is 0.9 of the main topmast. It would be possible to make it a proportion of the foremast, but this would cause difficulties because the foremast is stepped on the stem rather than the keel, so it is easier to use a proportion of the main topmast. This gives 30ft 8in.

The bowsprit should be almost as long as the foremast, with up to ¾ of its length projecting outside the hull. It is 51ft long.

### THE THICKNESSESS OF THE LOWER MASTS (G1)

Masts were circular in cross-section for most of their lengths. The diameter of a yard at the partners, where it meets the upper deck (or quarterdeck, in the case of the mizzen), should normally be 1/36 of the total length. Lees gives the following figures for the period before 1719:

| | |
|---|---|
| At the heel | 5/6 |
| First quarter | 42/43 |
| Second quarter | 14/15 |
| Third quarter | 5/6 |
| Hounds | 9/13 |
| Head | 4/7 |

For the *Susan Constant*, this gives:

| | Main | Fore | Mizzen |
|---|---|---|---|
| Heel | 17½in | 15in | 11¼in |
| Partners | 21in | 18in | 13½in |
| First quarter | 20½in | 17½in | 13¹⁄₆in |
| Second quarter | 19½in | 16⅔in | 12½in |

| | | | |
|---|---|---|---|
| Third quarter | 17½in | 15in | 11¼in |
| Hounds | 14½in | 12½in | 9¼in |
| Head | 12in | 10¼in | 7¾in |

## THE CONSTRUCTION OF THE LOWER MASTS (G4)

Masts on such a small ship would almost certainly be made from a single piece of timber. They would be circular in cross-section from the heel up to just below the hounds. The hounds came just under the trestletrees and were 'in effect the part of the cheek that was left flat under the trestle tree position' (Lees p 2). Each had a sheave set in it, for the ties of the yards. The length of the hound was two thirds of that of the masthead, which gives 3ft 9½in for the main, and 2ft 3.3in for the foremast. The head of the mast, above the hounds, was square in section, but with the corners rounded off. The heel in the lower end of the mast was cut in a tenon which fitted into the step. The mast between the partners and the hounds was 'wolded' (ropes would be wounded round it at intervals to help strengthen it). There would be about six or seven on each mast on a ship of this size. They would be 1ft wide, with wood 1½in wide above and below to keep them in place. The rope was one fifth the circumference of the mainstay, which was 10½in. Therefore, the woldings were 2in in circumference, or about ¾in in diameter (to the nearest ¼in). The mizzen would probably not be wolded. Using the same formulae as before, the head of the mizzen is 2ft 8½in, and the hounds are 1ft 9½in. Its hounds are octagonal, like those of the topmasts, and there is a single sheave for the tie of the yard, set fore and aft in the hounds.

## THE TOPMASTS (G6)

The lowest part of a topmast, the heel, is said to be 4ft in length, and is square in section. In practice, it has to be slightly less, or it will still be square where it meets the cap. Above the heel, the mast is circular until the hounds, which are octagonal in section. The head of the mast is square.

The lengths of the different parts are as follows:

| | Main topmast | Fore topmast |
|---|---|---|
| Heel | 3ft 6in | 3ft |
| Head, 1/10 of length | 3ft 3½in | 3ft 1in |
| Hounds, 1/20 of length | 1ft 7½in | 1ft 6½in |
| The thicknesses are | | |
| At cap, 15/16 per 3ft of length | 9½in | 9in |
| At lower head, 9/0 of diam at cap | 6⁷/₁₂in | 6¼in |
| At upper head, 11/20 of diam at cap | 5¼in | 5in |

According to Anderson, the thickness of the hounds should be half their depth. This gives: 10in 9in

A sheave for the toprope should be set athwartships 1ft from the lower end of the mast, with a groove running upwards to allow for the rope. The topmasts are not wolded.

There is no mizzen topmast, nor spritsail topmast.

## THE BOWSPRIT (G7)

The bowsprit has its thickest point where it meets the knightheads, just forward of the bulkhead of the forecastle. Its heel is angled to meet the deck, but its head is square. According to Anderson, the diameter at the knightheads should be equal to that of the foremast or slightly more. According to Lees, it should be equal to the diameter of the mainmast; the former has been chosen, giving a diameter of 18in. The diameters at other parts of the bowsprit are:

| | |
|---|---|
| Heel, ¾ of full diam | 13½in |
| *First* quarter, 30/31 full diam | 17½in |
| At head, ½ of full diam | 9in |

The bowsprit has cleats at various points to retain the gammoning and stays.

A ship of this size would not have had a spritsail topmast, and none of the prints studied shows a flagstaff on bowsprits on ships of this size.

## FLAGSTAFFS (G4)

The fore and main topmasts, and the mizzen mast should each have a flagstaff set above them. There is no specific information on their dimensions, but study of the Vischer print (Photograph 12) suggests about half the length of the topmast, with a rather shorter one on the mizzen. The lengths are therefore:

| | |
|---|---|
| Fore | 5ft 4in |
| Main | 16ft 6in |
| Mizzen | 12ft |

Presumably, they should be a little thinner, relative to their lengths, than the topmasts. Using the formula of 7/8in per 3ft of length, this gives:

| | |
|---|---|
| Fore | 4½in |
| Main | 5in |
| Mizzen | 3½in |

They should be half the diameter at the head, with a truck of the same diameter as the lower part. They are circular in section except for about 2ft at the heel, for joining with the trestletrees of the topmast or mizzen.

## CROSSTREES AND TRESTLETREES OF THE LOWER MASTS (G9, G10)

The lengths of the crosstrees and trestletrees for the fore and main lower masts are based on the diameters of the tops, as, according to Lees, the trees should come within an inch or two of the rim of the bottom of the top.

The diameter of the bottom of the top, according to figures given by Lees, should be:

| | |
|---|---|
| Main, 0.28 of topmast length | 9ft 3in |
| Fore, 0.29 of topmast length | 8ft 11in |

This does not convert easily to the actual length of the crosstrees and trestletrees, and it is necessary to draw them out to find exactly where they fit on the circle. To do that, it is necessary to find their approximate thicknesses. Anderson says the width of the trestletrees should be about 7/8 or 9/10 of their depth, which should be 1/13 of their length. Using 9/10 gives the following figures:

| | Main | Fore |
|---|---|---|
| Depth | 8½in | 8¼in |
| Width | 7½in | 7½in |

The crosstrees have the same width as the trestletrees, and half the depth (4¼in on each). Space has to be left between the trees for the head of the lower mast, and the heel of the topmast. The trestletrees have recesses to fit round the mast, to a depth of 1/8 of their width – 1in. There is a chock between the head of the lower mast and the heel of the topmast, of the same width and depth as the trestletree.

In profile, the outer quarters of the crosstrees and trestletrees taper upwards until the depth is halved. They have their ends rounded off in plan. The crosstrees are recessed into the trestletrees to a depth of about ¾in less than their own depth – 3¾in. A bolster is placed over the top of each trestletree at the side of the lower masthead, to guide the shrouds. The bolster forms a quadrant of a circle in cross-section, and in depth and height it is equal to the width of the trestle, less the rebate for the mast – 6½in for both fore and main. It should extend a little way forward and aft of the mast position.

## TRESTLETREES AND CROSSTREES FOR THE UPPER MASTS AND MIZZEN (G11)

There are few specific dimensions for the trees of the upper masts, but they need much less strength than the lower ones, as they only have to bear flagstaffs rather than masts. They are proportional to the size of the appropriate flagstaff, in the same way as the lower ones are proportional to the topmasts, using an imaginary top to give the length. In the case of the mizzen, the relative thickness of the masthead compared with the flagstaff requires a slight difference – the trees are taken right out to the imaginary top, instead of 1in in from it. The dimensions are as follows:

|  | Fore | Main | Mizzen |
|---|---|---|---|
| Diam of top | 4ft 3½in | 4ft 7½in | 3ft 4½in |
| Width of trestletree and crosstree | 3½in | 3¾in | 2¾in |
| Depth of trestletree | 4in | 4¼in | 3in |
| Depth of crosstree | 2in | 2in | 1½in |
| Length of crosstree | 3ft 9in | 4ft | 2ft 11½in |
| Length of trestletree | 3ft 11½in | 4ft 3½in | 3ft 2½in |
| Recess for trestletree | ¾in | ¾in | ¾in |
| Recess for crosstree | 1¼in | 1¼in | ¾in |

The crosstrees of these masts should not be tapered, as they will become unduly thin.

## CAPS (G12)

The head of a lower mast is held to the partners of the upper mast by means of a cuboid piece of timber known as a cap, bored with a round hole for the upper mast, and a square one for the lower. Lees gives the following dimensions:

| Length | 4 × diam of round hole |
|---|---|
| Width | 2 × diam of round hole |
| Depth | Diam of round hole |

Obviously, the distance between the centres of the masts is the same at the cap as at the trestletrees. The following dimensions can be calculated from the above:

|  | Fore | Main | Mizzen | Fore topmast | Main topmast |
|---|---|---|---|---|---|
| Distance between centres of holes | 1ft 6¼in | 1ft 7½in | 9.15in | 9½in | 9¾in |
| Diam of round hole | 9in | 9½in | 3½in | 4½in | 5in |
| Side of square hole | 10¾in | 12in | 7¾in | 5in | 5¼in |
| Total length | 3ft | 3ft 2in | 1ft 2in | 1ft 6in | 1ft 8in |
| Width | 1ft 6in | 1ft 7in | 7in | 9in | 10in |
| Depth | 9in | 9½in | 3½in | 4½in | 5in |

## TOPS (G13, G14, G15, G16)

The diameters of the tops have already been calculated. There is a square hole in the middle of each top. Anderson says that this should be 2/5 or 1/3 of the diameter of the top; the latter is used. The base is made up of planks running parallel to the sides of the hole. According to Lees, they should be 2½in thick and 6in broad. They are cut to half this thickness at the ends, and should overlap. Above the outer edge of the base, was fixed the rim, 6in wide, 1in deep, and probably made in eight sections.

Radiating from the centre of the top were the battens or knees. Lees suggests that they should be about 18in apart at their outer ends, so this means a total of 20, set at angles of 18 degrees to one another. They are about 2in wide. Lees says each rib should be made in three parts, scarfed together. Each rib follows the line of the base, then turns upwards at about 45 degrees, to form the side of the top, which is planked over with 1in plank. Lees seems to imply three strakes of 4in plank, adding up to 12in on the diagonal. At the top of the planking is another rim, into which the ends of the ribs are tenoned. It has the same dimensions as the lower rim, 6in wide and 1in deep. Above this rail are vertical posts, which support another rail, about 4in wide, with its outer edge on a level with the rim below. It is also 1in thick.

## THE LENGTHS OF THE YARDS

Anderson provides a method of calculating the lengths of the yards, but this produces a very large sail plan. Therefore, the method given by Mainwaring (p 259) is used. The lengths of the yards are as follows:

| Fore | 36ft 9½in |
|---|---|
| Main | 46ft |
| Mizzen | 36ft 9½in |
| Fore topsail | 15ft 9in |
| Main topsail | 19ft 8½in |
| Spritsail | 25ft 10in |

## SHAPE OF THE YARDS (G18, G19)

The five square yards are all essentially the same shape, with diameters in proportion to their lengths. All are round in cross-section throughout their lengths. Using the system described by Anderson, their diameters are as follows:

|  | Foreyard | Mainyard | Main topsail | Fore topsail | Spritsail |
|---|---|---|---|---|---|
| Diam at slings (1/48 of length) | 9.2in | 11½in | 4.9in | 3.9in | 6½in |
| First quarter (23/24 of slings) | 8.8in | 11in | 4.7in | 3.7in | 6.2in |
| Second quarter (6/7 of slings) | 7.9in | 9.9in | 4.2in | 3.3in | 5.6in |
| Third quarter (2/3 of slings) | 6.1in | 7.7in | 3.3in | 2.6in | 4.3in |
| Yardarm (1/3 of slings) | 3in | 3.8in | 1.6in | 1.3in | 2.2in |

The square yards also have certain fittings – sling cleats near the centre, robband strips just outside, and several cleats at the end of the yardarm. There is some doubt about how many yardarm cleats were fitted, but Lees is followed in having four on each yardarm. The yardarm cleats are on the top and bottom of the yard, the sling cleats on the top only, and the robband strip is on the forward face. The dimensions and positions of the various cleats are as follows:

| | Foreyard | Mainyard | Main topsail | Fore topsail | Spritsail |
|---|---|---|---|---|---|
| Length of sling cleats (1/20 of total) | 22in | 27½in | 12in | 9½in | 15.5in |
| Length of shoulder (1/3 of cleat) | 7.3in | 9in | 4in | 3.1in | 5.2in |
| Breadth[1] (¼ length) | 5½in | 6.9in | 3in | 2.4in | 3.9in |
| Depth (2/3 breadth) | 3.7in | 4.3in | 2in | 1.6in | 2.6in |
| Gap between cleats (¼ of diam of yard) | 2.3in | 2.9in | 1.2in | 1in | 1.6in |
| Length of robband strip (1/8 of length of yard) | 55in | 69in | 30in | 24in | 39in |
| Gap between strips (½ length of one strip) | 27½in | 34½in | 15in | 12in | 19½in |
| Length of yardarm cleats (½ diam of yard) | 4.6in | 5¾in | 2½in | 2in | 3¼in |
| Breadth (¼ length) | 1.2in | 1.4in | 0.6in | ½in | 0.8in |
| Thickness (2/3 breadth) | 0.8in | 0.9in | ½in[2] | ½in[2] | ½in |
| Distance of innermost cleat from end of yard (1/24 of length of yard) | 18.4in | 23in | 9.8in | 7.8in | 23in |
| Distance between (1/7 of above) | 2.6in | 3.2in | 1.4in | 1.2in | 3.2in |

[1] Depth is assumed to be the same as for the sling cleats, breadth is half that.
[2] This dimension would be too small if taken from the formula, so is increased slightly.

The ends of the yards are rounded.

## THE MIZZENYARD (G20)

The mizzenyard differs from the others in that its slings are not in the middle, but are 1/22 of the length of the yard forward of the middle (20in). The diameter is calculated as with the other yards, and is 9.2in. The forward (lower) arm should taper to a half at the end, and the after (upper) arm to two thirds. This gives 4.6in, and 6.1in. The yardarm cleats are the same as those of the foreyard. They are fitted to the port and starboard sides of the yard, instead of the top and bottom. The sling cleats are also the same as those of the foreyard, but fitted to the starboard side instead of the upper part. They are one diameter of the yard apart. There are no robband strips.

# Standing rigging

## THE PENDANTS (H1, H4)

At the masthead, the pendants are fitted first. These are ropes with a block on the end, used mainly for lifting heavy weights into the ship; they are the same diameter as the shrouds, with enough length to take them about half way down the mast. There is one on each side of each mast and topmast, and are spliced together with a double eyesplice. Presumably, when not in use, they were hauled up to the top and stowed there, rather than left hanging.

## THE SHROUDS (H1, H2, H4)

Based mainly on the evidence of the Vischer print of 1610 (Photograph 12), the mainmast and the foremast have been given five shrouds on each side, while the mizzen has three. The two topmasts also have three each. The first pair of shrouds on one side are seized together, leaving a loop just big enough to fit over the masthead, and then passed over the masthead. The same is done with the first pair on the opposite side, and so on. There is an odd number on each mast, so the last one on each side has an eye splice. After fitting, they sit one above another on the masthead. The foremost shroud on each mast would be wormed and served, while the others are wormed, but only served in the part that goes round the masthead.

## DEADEYES AND CHANNELS (H5)

The lower end of each shroud is seized round the upper deadeye. The deadeye itself should presumably be round, as heart shaped deadeyes had gone out of use by that time. Its face was also quite rounded, compared to those used in later years which were flatter. It was fitted by means of a lanyard to the lower deadeye, which was fitted to the channels or the top. Each deadeye has three holes, and the lanyard is passed from one to the other, the end being tied round the lower part of the shroud.

Each shroud was turned round its upper deadeye, in the groove provided for this. At the top of the deadeye, the two ends were crossed over, and the shorter one was seized to the longer one. One end of the lanyard was finished off with a knot (figure-of-eight or Matthew Walker), and the rest of it passed through the holes in alternate deadeyes. The remaining end was then turned round the shroud above the deadeye a few times, and seized to it.

The lower deadeye had an iron strap round it, with a small loop in the bottom. The chain plate was basically a strip of iron, with a hook at one end, which passed through the loop in the strap. The lower end was shaped to take a bolt, which passed through the side of the ship at the level of the lower channel wale.

## FUTTOCK SHROUDS AND THEIR FITTING (H6)

The futtock stave was a piece of timber lashed outside the shrouds, to help hold the futtock shrouds. The lower end of the futtock shroud was turned round the stave, then lashed to the shroud below. The upper end was seized to a hook, which was placed through the chain plate. The chain plate went up through the upper rim of the top, being fitted at a suitable angle to keep the futtock shroud clear of the side of the top. The chain plate was looped round the lower deadeye of the topmast shrouds, as with the deadeyes of the courses.

## CATHARPINS (H1, H7)

The upper catharpins are fitted at the level of the futtock staves, on the main and foremasts. A line is seized to the first shroud, then led through a hole in a deadeye, back to the second shroud, through the next hole in the deadeye, back to the third shroud, and so on. The deadeye is lashed to a block, and this is held to the corresponding block on the other side by an arrangement of tackles.

The lower catharpins are at about two thirds of the way down the shrouds. A block is lashed to each shroud at this level, and a line is led through each block on alternate sides, with both ends being led down and belayed on the deck. Evidently, they were only used on the fore and main lower masts, and perhaps they were not fitted at all times.

## RATLINES (H8)

All shrouds, including futtock shrouds, are fitted with ratlines. On the main and foremasts, only one in six goes as far back as the aftermost shroud, which is known as the swifter. The ratlines are fixed to the shrouds by means of clove hitches. (In later years, they would be fixed to the end shrouds by eyesplice and seizing, but this method does not seem to have been used in 1607.) The shrouds are 15in apart.

## BACKSTAYS (H2)

In this period, backstays were only fitted on the fore and main topmasts, one on each side. The pendant came down as far as the level of the top, where a block was fitted. The fall was passed through the block, with each end fitted at a timberhead on the side of the hull. The following table shows the dimensions of the ropes, blocks, etc, connected with the shrouds, based on the formulae given by Lees:

| | Foremast | Mainmast | Mizzen | Fore topmast | Main topmast |
|---|---|---|---|---|---|
| Circ of shroud | 5½in | 6¼in | 5½in | 3¾in | 4in |
| Diam of deadeye | 9in | 10in | 9in | 6in | 6½in |
| Circ of lanyard | 2¾in | 3¼in | 2¾in | 2in | 2in |
| Circ of catharpins | 1¾in | 1¾in | 1¾in | 1in | 1in |
| Diam of catharpin blocks | 7in | 7in | 7in | 4in | 4in |
| Diam of catharpin deadeyes | 3in | 3in | 3in | 1¾in | 1¾in |
| Circ of ratlines | 1½in | 1½in | 1½in | 1½in | 1½in |
| Size of pendant block | 14½in | 17¼in | 14½in | 10in | 10½in |
| Circ of backstay pendant | – | – | – | 2¾in | 3in |
| Circ of backstay fall | – | – | – | 1¾in | 2in |
| Length of backstay block | – | – | – | 7in | 8in |

## STAYS (H2)

Stays lead forward from the appropriate mast to the deck, or to another spar. In later years, the upper end of the stay would be formed into a loop by means of a system known as the mouse and collar, but Anderson provides considerable evidence that this system was not in use in the 1600s, and a simple eyesplice was used. This was looped over the masthead after all the shrouds and pendants had been fitted. Stays were wormed, parcelled and served along their whole length. The leads of the various stays were as follows:

*Forestay*: from the head of the foremast to a position about half way along the exposed part of the bowsprit.
*Mainstay*: from the head of the mainmast to the top of the stem. The collar is very long, and extends aft so that it meets the stay proper behind the foremast.
*Mizzenstay*: from the head of the mizzenmast, to a collar which is lashed round the mainmast a few feet above the deck.
*Foretopmast stay*: from the head of the foretopmast to a position near the end of the bowsprit.
*Maintopmast stay*: from the head of the maintopmast to the head of the foremast, just above the top.

At this period, the stay was linked to the collar by means of a pair of deadeyes, not hearts as were used later. Therefore each stay has a deadeye seized to its lower end, except the foretopmast stay, which has a block.

## COLLARS OF STAYS (H10)

A typical collar was wormed, parcelled and served. It was seized round the deadeye, and each end was then finished with an eyesplice. The two ends were placed round the appropriate master stay, and lashed together. The foretopmast stay had a rather different arrangement: a rope was fixed round the outer end of the bowsprit, then taken through the block at the end of the stay, and to another block. Another rope was seized round the bowsprit a few feet further in, through the block in the first rope, and then through another block seized to the bowsprit. After that, it was led along the bowsprit to the deck, where it was belayed forward of the forecastle bulkhead. The blocks would be 9in in length, and the ropes going through them would be 2¼in in circumference.

The following table gives the dimensions of stays, deadeyes, collars and lanyards:

| | Main | Fore | Mizzen | Fore topmast | Main topmast |
|---|---|---|---|---|---|
| Circ of stay | 10½in | 9in | 6¾in | 4½in | 4¾in |
| Diam of deadeye | 17in | 14½in | 11in | – | 7¾in |
| Circ of collar | 9½in | 8¼in | 6¼in | – | 3¾in |
| Circ of lanyards | 3½in | 3in | 2¼in | 2¼in | 2½in |

## GAMMONING OF BOWSPRIT (H11)

The only standing rigging on the bowsprit is the gammoning. This is turned round the bowsprit itself, then through a specially placed hole in the upper part of the knee to the head. About ten turns are taken, from after on the bowsprit to forward in the gammoning hole, so that it twists through 180 degrees. The whole system is kept tight by turning the end of the rope about ten times round the central part of the gammoning. The circumference of the gammoning is 4¾in.

# SAILS

## THE SHAPES OF THE SAILS

The foresail and mainsail are parallel sided, and are rectangular except that a hollowing, or roach, is cut out of the middle of the lower edge, to allow the sails to clear the decks. The spritsail is rectangular. The two topsails have no roach, but taper upwards to match the sizes of their yards. The mizzen sail could be triangular, but this does not fit the shape provided for it, so it is carried down a few feet by a parallel-sided section.

All sails have a certain amount of 'bag' – that is, they are not completely flat surfaces, but are taken in round their edges, so that the sail forms a rounded shape when filled with wind. Anderson suggests that in the eighteenth century, the practice was to take in 1/12 at the head and foot of the sail, and 1/24 at the leech. However, seventeenth-century sails, invariably, have a baggier appearance, so these amounts should be increased; in the absence of any specific information, they should be 1/9 and 1/18, respectively.

The fore, main, and mizzen sails (the courses) are all divided into two parts; the sail proper, and the bonnet, which is laced under the sail, and is removable in strong winds. This provides a system of reefing, as reef points were not in use at this time. The bonnet is made as part of the sail in the first instance, then cut off and fitted with its own head rope, etc. This ensures that it has the same bag as the sail proper. The mizzen bonnet is cut so that the sail proper is triangular, and the bonnet is quadrilateral.

## THE SIZES OF THE SAILS (I1)

The heads of sails are, of course, smaller than the yards to which they are attached. Since they were lashed to the yardarm cleats, the length of the yardarm has always to be deducted. A further 12in, or so, is also deducted on each side, as the sail is hauled out to the yardarm cleat.

The fore and main courses are parallel sided, so the width at the foot is the same as at the head. The spritsail is similar. The width of the foot of the topsails are equal to the distance between the yardarm cleats, with perhaps a deduction of about 18in on each side to help stretch the sail between the sheet blocks.

The depth of each sail is determined by suspending the yard a few feet under the sheaves in the hounds of the mast, and measuring the distance to the deck, or the yard, below. In the case of the courses, some room has to be left to clear the deck.

The mizzen is drawn by placing the mizzen yard some distance below the hounds, with the slings just forward of the mast. It hangs at an angle roughly parallel to the mizzen stay. A line is drawn parallel to the deck, from the lowest yardarm cleat, and this, together with a vertical drawn down from the upper yardarm, determines the shape of the sail without the bonnet. The bonnet is shaped by drawing another line parallel to the lower edge of the sail, at a sufficient height to clear the deck. The aftermost vertical is extended to meet it, and the fore edge is formed by another line parallel to that.

The sizes of the sails, including bonnets, are as follows:

| | Fore | Main | Fore topsail | Main topsail | Sprit-sail | Mizzen |
|---|---|---|---|---|---|---|
| Head | 30ft 10½in | 40ft 2in | 12ft 5in | 16ft ½in | 22ft | 30ft 10½in |
| Foot | – | – | 29ft 10½in | 39ft 6in | – | 20ft 4in |
| Total depth | 32ft 3in | 34ft 2½in | 28ft 10in | 32ft 1in | 14ft 9in | 31ft 4in |
| Depth of roach | 3ft 6in | 4ft | – | – | – | – |
| Depth of luff | | | – | – | – | 9ft 7in |

## SAILMAKING (I2, I3, I4, I5)

As far as we know, sails were made in 2ft strips sewn together, with some overlap. Obviously, this overlap would have to be greater at the head and foot, to create the bag – or else the width of the sail could be trimmed so that the sides were no longer parallel. Assuming a minimum overlap of 1½in, this should be increased to 1 11/18in in the middle of each seam. However, the sails are drawn out as if they were flat.

Sails have lining – an extra thickness of cloth – at certain parts where they are subject to wear. The outermost cloths on the fore and main courses are doubled in this manner. Likewise the fore and main topsails have a doubling in their central part, to protect them from the tops. The spritsail has two rows of doubling, crossed over in the middle of the sail. The mizzen sail is doubled for parts of its leech, and its bonnet is doubled on both luff and leech.

Each sail has a 'tabling' or hemming round all its edges. It is on the after side of the sail on all square sails. The ends and edges of the cloth are simply turned over and sewn down. The width of the tabling, according to Lees, is as follows:

| | Courses | Topsails and spritsails | Mizzen |
|---|---|---|---|
| Head | 4in | 3in | 3in |
| Leech and foot | 3in | 3in | 3in (leech) 2in (foot) |
| Luff | – | – | 3½in |

Ropes, collectively known as bolt ropes, are sewn round the sail to strengthen them. The leech and foot ropes are the same size, while the head rope is smaller. The circumferences are as follows:

| | Leech and foot ropes | Head |
|---|---|---|
| Fore course | 3in | 1¼in |
| Main course | 3½in | 1½in |
| Mizzen | 3½in | 1¾in |
| Foretopsail | 3in | 1¼in |
| Maintopsail | 3in | 1¼in |
| Spritsail | 2in | 1in |

## THE BONNETS (I1, I2, I5, I6)

The depth of the mizzen bonnet is largely determined by the shape of the sail. The depth of the fore and main bonnets are 4/13 of the sail; this gives 9ft 11in for the fore bonnet, and 10ft 6in for the main.

The bonnet is fitted with a headrope and tabling as with the sail, while the sail above has the appropriate footrope and tabling. The top edge of the bonnet and the lower edge of the sail are cut with holes through the tabling, one for each seam. A short rope, with a wall knot in the end, is fitted to each upper corner of the bonnet; presumably this leads through the clew cringles of the sail. The sail and bonnet are laced together by a complex system of ropes leading through both sets of holes. The exact details of this are not clear.

## EARRINGS (I2)

At each corner of a square sail is an earring, formed out of the same rope as the leech rope. It serves to hold the appropriate rigging. The clew earring, at the bottom corner, is made by forming a loop in the leech rope as it turns the corner and forms the footrope; it is seized round its throat. The head earring, at the top corner, is formed by turning the leechline back on itself and sewing the end onto the sail.

## CRINGLES (I2, I3, I4, I5, I7)

A cringle is a small loop of rope used for attaching a rope to a sail at a specific point. They were about half an inch smaller than the appropriate leech rope. The fore and main courses have, on the leeches, six martnet cringles, quite close together in the top half, and two bowline cringles in the bottom half. The foot has three buntline cringles. The bonnets have no cringles. The topsails have two bowline cringles on each leech, in the lower half, and two buntline cringles on the foot. The mizzen has six martnet cringles on its leech, and three buntline cringles on the foot. The spritsail has one cringle low down on each leech, at the level where the lining meets the leech. These are used for the leech tackle. It also has two buntline cringles on the foot.

## ATTACHING THE SAIL TO THE YARD (I7)

The sail is attached to the yard by means of ropes known as rope-bands, or robbands, passed through holes in the tabling of the head. There are normally two holes in each cloth. The robbands are passed over the top of the yard, and secured by a simple reef knot above the yard. A rope is passed through the head earring, and several turns are taken round the top of the yard, and through the earring again. It is then passed over the yard between the yardarm cleats, to help stretch the sail.

# RUNNING RIGGING

## TIES, HALYARDS AND RUNNERS (J1, J2, J3, J4)

The fore and mainyards are hoisted by means of ties. Each tie is fixed round the centre of the yard between the sling cleats. It is led through one of the sheaves set in the hounds of the mast, and then down to the 'ramshead' block. It is passed through a hole in the block, and back up through the other sheave in the hounds. A preventer rope is used to tie the two parts of the tie together near the ramshead, to stop the block from hitting the mast if the yard is suddenly let go.

The ramshead is a treble block, and the halyard connects it to a knighthead set in the deck just aft of the mast. The knighthead has four sheaves, three of which are used for the halyard. One end of the halyard is seized to the side of the knighthead, and then led alternately through the sheaves of the ramshead and the knighthead. The other end is hitched round the knighthead.

With the topmasts, the tie is single. It is fixed round the centre of the yard, and then through the sheave in the hounds of the topmast, ending in a single block, to take the halyard. The runner was seized to an eyebolt on the starboard side of the deck, and then went through the lift block and back to the deck where it was belayed.

The mizzen tie was also fitted round the thickest part of the yard, between the sling cleats. It was led through the sheave in the hounds, and ended in a single block. The fall or halyard was attached to this block, and was led through the first of two sheaves in the mizzen knighthead, back through the first block, and then through the second sheave in the knighthead.

In each case, the tie must be long enough to allow the mast to be lowered either to the deck or to the appropriate top, without taking the block too close to the sheave in the hounds of the mast.

The spritsail halyard was fitted to the end of the bowsprit by an eyesplice. It was led through a single block in the slings of the yard, through another single block at the end of the bowsprit, then to the head range.

The truss, or downhaul, was used to haul the lower yards down to the deck. There is no specific information on its dimensions, but presumably it was smaller than the ties – perhaps about half. It was hitched round the centre of the main or foreyard, and then taken straight down to the deck, where it was presumably belayed when not in use.

The sizes of the appropriate ropes and blocks are:

| | Fore | Main | Mizzen | Main topsail | Fore topsail | Sprit-sail |
|---|---|---|---|---|---|---|
| Tie | 4½in | 5¼in | 3¾in | 4in | 3¾in | |
| Ramshed or runner block | 14in | 16in | 12in | 14in | 15in | 14in |
| Halyard or runner | 3½in | 4in | 3in | 3½in | 3¼in | 3½in |
| Preventer | 2¼in | 2¾in | | | | |

## PARRELS (J5, J6)

All the yards, including the mizzen and spritsail, are held to the mast by means of parrels. A parrel is an arrangement of ribs and trucks, intended to allow the yard to rotate, or be raised and lowered as necessary. Since the yard was often lowered to the deck to furl the sail, the parrel rope has to lead down to the deck so that it can be used easily. The main and fore parrels have three rows of trucks. The topsail, mizzen, and spritsail parrels have only two.

The dimensions of the parts of the parrels are as follows:

| | Fore | Main | Mizzen | Fore topsail | Main topsail | Sprit-sail |
|---|---|---|---|---|---|---|
| Parrel rope | 3in | 3½in | 3½in | 3in | 3in | 3in |
| Diam of truck | 4½in | 5¼in | 5¼in | 4½in | 4½in | 4½in |
| Length of truck | 5¾in | 6½in | 6½in | 5¾in | 5¾in | 5¾in |
| Length of rib | 24in | 28in | 19in | 17in | 17in | 17in |

## LIFTS (J7, J8, J9)

Lifts are used to support the ends of yards, and keep them level. In the case of the fore and mainyards, one end of the lift is seized to the collar of the stay, just under the top. It then leads through a single block at the yardarm (seized to the topsail sheet block, which is also at the yardarm). The lift then goes through another single block, hung under the top by means of a long strop going round the mast head, over the tops of the shrouds, collar, etc. The lift is then led to the deck.

The topsail lifts begin at the topsail cap. An arrangement of rope known as a span is fitted round the cap, between the flagstaff and the topmast. It is simply a piece of rope with an eyesplice in each end, clove hitched round the cap. The end of the lift is seized to the eyesplice in the end of the cap. It is led through the block in the end of the yard, then through another under the trestletrees (fitted in the same way as that under the lower top), and led down to the deck.

It is not possible to lead the mizzen lift to the mizzen topmast, as that is far too low, and the flagstaff is not designed for such loads. Therefore, the lift is led to the main topmast head. At the peak of the mizzen yard, the lift is divided into two parts by means of a block (a more complex system is shown on most drawings, but the simpler system is appropriate to such a small ship). The lift is led to a block hung from the main topmast head, and then led back to a block at the mizzen masthead, and down to belay at the deck.

The spritsail lift is seized to a block at the head of the bowsprit. It runs through another block at the yardarm of the spritsail yard, then through the first block, and back to the foredeck.

The sizes of the ropes and blocks are as follows:

| | Fore | Main | topsail | Fore topsail | Main Mizzen | Sprit-sail |
|---|---|---|---|---|---|---|
| Lifts | 3in | 3½in | 3¼in | 3½in | 2¼in | 2in |
| Lift blocks | 12in | 14in | 13in | 14in | 9in | 8in |

## FITTINGS ON CLEWS (J10, J11)

The lower corners, or clews, of the foresail, have to hold three ropes – the sheet, tack and clew garnet. All have to be easily removable, so that they can be transferred to the bonnet or the sail proper as required. The clew garnet block is fitted with an endless strop. It is passed over the clew earring of the sail, and then the block is passed through the hole. The sheet block has two ends to its strop, each with a wall knot, while the tack ends in a large wall knot. All these are passed through the lower part of the clew earring, and a seizing is taken round the earring just above these ropes, to hold them in place. If the bonnet is removed, the seizing is taken off and the three blocks are transferred to the sail proper.

The topsail clews are slightly simpler, in that there are no tacks, and no bonnet. The strop of the clewline block is looped over the clew earring, and then the sheet, which has a wall knot in its end, is passed through.

## SHEETS (J12, J13, J14, J15)

The sheets of the lower square sails, the fore, main and spritsail, all lead aft from the sail to positions on the side of the hull. The main sheet begins at an eyebolt fixed to the outside of the hull just forward of the quarter gallery. It leads through a block in the clew of the sail, then back through a sheave in the side of the hull, just above the first block, just above the level of the quarter deck. Other leads are possible, but this one has the advantage that the end of the sheet is kept above decks, where it is easier to control, and does not interfere with accommodation below.

The foresheet starts at an eyebolt in the side, a few feet forward of the main channels. It leads through a block in the clew of the sail, and back through a sheave in the side of the ship, above the first block, and at the level of the upper deck.

Unlike the first two, the spritsail sheet has a long pendant, extending as far aft as the main channels. The sheet begins just forward of, and lower than, the foresheet, at the level of the lower channel wale. It leads through a block in the end of the pendant, and back through another sheave at upper deck level.

The topsail sheets are rather different in function. They merely serve to hold the clews close to the ends of the lower yards. Each sheet is taken through the sheet block, at the yardarm, then along the after side of the yard to another block hung under the yard, near the robband strip. The sheet is then taken down to the deck.

The end of the mizzen sheet is fixed to an eyebolt inside the transom. It goes through a block in the clew of the sail, and down to another block fixed just under the eyebolt. From there, it is belayed on a cleat well aft on the inside of the ship.

The sizes of ropes and blocks are as follows:

| | Fore | Main | Mizzen | Fore topsail | Main topsail | Sprit-sail |
|---|---|---|---|---|---|---|
| Sheet | 3¾in | 4¼in | 4½in | 4in | 4¼in | 2¼in |
| Pendant | | | | | | 3½in |
| Blocks | 15in | 17in | 18in | 16in | 17in | 9in |
| Length of pendant | | | | | | 33ft |

## TACKS (J12, J13, J14, J15)

The main tack is a single rope leading from the clew of the main course through a sheave in the side of the hull just aft of the forecastle bulkhead. The fore tack leads from the clew to a hole in the knee of the head, and then back to the forecastle, to belay on the opposite side of the ship. Presumably it is taken through the deck of the beakhead.

| | Fore | Main |
|---|---|---|
| Circumference of tack | 5½in | 6½in |

The mizzen tack is only needed when the bonnet is in use. It is a single rope, fixed to the lower forward earring of the sail, and led to an eyebolt at one side or the other of the quarterdeck, according to which tack the ship is sailing on. It is 4in in circumference.

## BRACES (J12, J13, J14, J15)

The main braces each have a pendant. One end is seized to the yardarm, and the other has a single block. The brace begins at an eyebolt on the side of the ship well aft at quarterdeck level, and then goes through the block, and back to an eyebolt on the rail of the quarterdeck, and down to belay on the side.

The forebraces also have pendants. Each brace begins about a third of the way up the mainstay, and through the pendant block, back to a block fixed to the stay a little way below where the end of the brace is seized, and then down to belay at the side of the ship just aft of the forecastle bulkhead.

The main topsail brace has a pendant, with a single block. The brace is seized under the mizzen trestletrees, and goes up through the pendant block. It then leads down to a block fitted about two thirds of the way up the foremost mizzen shroud, then forward to another block seized to the aftermost main shroud, and down to belay on deck.

The foretopsail brace starts on the main topmast stay, goes through the pendant block, back to another block seized to the main topmast stay just below where the end of the brace is seized; and then through another block seized to the mainstay, and down to belay on the deck.

The spritsail braces are seized halfway up to the forestay. Each goes through a block with a short pendant, attached to the yardarm, and back to a block on the forestay, then down to belay on the foredeck. The sizes are as follows:

| | Fore | Main | Fore topsail | Main topsail | Sprit-sail |
|---|---|---|---|---|---|
| Circ of brace | 1¾in | 2in | 1½in | 1½in | 2½in |
| Circ of pendant | 3in | 3½in | 2in | 2¼in | 2¾in |
| Length of blocks | 7in | 8in | 6in | 6in | 9in |
| Length of pendants | 11ft | 14ft | 5ft | 6ft | 3ft |

## BOWLINES (J12, J13, J14, J15)

On a small ship like this, each bowline had two bridles, leading to the leech of the sail. It seems likely that when the bonnet was in use, the lower leg of the bridle was transferred to the clew earring of the sail.

One end of the bridle is attached to the cringle on the sail by means of a bowline knot. It is led through a loop in the end of the bowline, and then is tied to the other cringle on the sail.

The main bowline leads to a block about half way long the bowsprit, and then down to the forecastle, through the gammoning block. The fore bowline leads to a block on the bowsprit, just aft of the forestay collar. It then leads through the gammoning block, and to the foredeck.

Both the main topsail bowlines lead to a double block seized to the maintopmast stay, and then to another double block seized to the mast just below the hounds, and down to the deck. The foretopsail bowline goes through a block seized to the foretopmast stay at the level of the top; it then goes down to another block seized to the bowsprit just forward of the forestay collar, and to the foredeck via the gammoning block.

| | Fore | Main | Fore topsail | Main topsail |
|---|---|---|---|---|
| Circumference of bowlines and bridles | 2¼in | 2¾in | 2in | 2¼in |
| Length of blocks | 9in | 11in | 8in | 9in |

Again, the mizzen bowlines are different from the others. There is one on each side, leading from the forward yardarm cleats to a block on the after main shroud, and down to belay on the deck. They are 4½in in circumference, and the blocks are 18in long.

## BUNTLINES (J18, J19, J20, J21)

All sails have buntlines, though on the mizzen stay they are more commonly known as brails. The buntlines lift the foot of the sail when it is furled, and are attached to cringles. There is some doubt about the exact form of the fore and main course buntlines, but it seems most likely that there were three cringles on the foot of the sail. One line led from each, and they joined together a small distance up from there. The single line thus formed was taken up the fore side of the sail, through a block suspended from the collar of the main or forestay. It then went down to belay on the deck.

The topsail buntlines were probably two in number, leading from buntline cringles at the foot of the sail, through a block under the yard, and then through another suspended from the cap of the topmast, and down to belay at the deck.

The mizzen buntlines, like those of the courses, are divided into two parts; once they have joined, the single line goes through a block attached to the forward part of the mizzen yard, and then down to the rail at the side of the ship. The mizzen has buntlines on both sides of the sail, whereas the other sails have them on the fore side only.

The spritsail buntline is a single rope, beginning at a cringle at the centre of the foot of the sail. It leads through a block attached to the bowsprit just forward of the spritsail yard, and belays on the foredeck.

| | Fore | Main | Mizzen | Main topsail | Fore topsail | Sprit-sail |
|---|---|---|---|---|---|---|
| Circ of buntline | 1¾in | 2in | 3½in | 1¾in | 2in | 2in |
| Length of blocks | 7in | 8in | 14in | 7in | 8in | 8in |

## MARTNETS (J18, J20)

Martnets are fitted to the lower sails only. They are fitted both fore and aft of the sail. Larger ships had twelve legs on each set, but it seems more likely that a small ship like the *Susan Constant* would only have six. The legs are fitted to cringles in the leech of the sail, and join together at a deadeye. The rope attached to the deadeye leads to a block hung by a long pendant from the cap of the mast, and then it goes down to the deck.

| | Fore | Main | Mizzen |
|---|---|---|---|
| Circ of legs | 1¾in | 2in | 1¾in |
| Circ of falls | 1½in | 1¾in | 1¾in |
| Diam of deadeye | 3in | 3½in | 2¾in |
| Length of blocks | 7in | 8in | 7in |

## CLEWLINES (J18, J19, J21)

Clewlines are fitted on all the square sails, on the after side. They serve to pull the lower corner of the sail into the centre of the yard, for furling. A clewgarnet of the main or foresail begins about a third of the way out from the centre of the yard, where it is seized. It goes through a block fixed to the clew of the sail, as described above, and then through another block fitted to the yard just inboard of the first block. It goes down to the deck to belay at the bitts. Clewlines of the topsails are similar, but go down to the deck via the lubber's hole in the top. The clewlines of the spritsail belay on the foredeck. Dimensions are:

| | Fore | Main | Fore topsail | Main topsail | Sprit-sail |
|---|---|---|---|---|---|
| Circ of clewline or garnet | 1¾in | 2in | 2in | 2¼in | 1¾in |
| Length of blocks | 7in | 8in | 8in | 9in | 7in |

## THE GAMMONING BLOCK (J22)

The gammoning blocks are lashed to the gammoning of the bowsprit on each side, and help to lead the ropes going to the forward rail of the forecastle. They are long blocks, consisting of several sheaves placed one above another, with the shell of the block made as one piece. Seven ropes are involved, so the port gammoning block has three sheaves, and the starboard one has four.

## TYPES OF BELAYING POINTS (J23, J24, J25, J26, J27)

In dealing with belaying points, the standard authorities are often unspecific and contradictory. This merely reflects the fact that there was no standard system, and that captains and ship designers each had different ideas.

It cannot be assumed that all the nineteenth-century forms of belaying points were in use in the early seventeenth century. However, the study of contemporary sources tends to confirm that most were used in one form or another.

Racks of belaying pins were not known as such, but both Mainwaring and Boteler mention 'ranges', which were rather like small versions of the main pitts, with two verticals and a horizontal piece. Each horizontal had 'divers wooden pins through it, to belay ropes unto' (Mainwaring p 207). These were the forerunners of the belaying pin, though it cannot be assumed that they had the characteristic shape. There were only two of these ranges, one aft of the foremast and one on the beakhead, 'before the woldings of the bowsprit'. Mainwaring mentions various ropes which are fitted to these ranges, including most of those of the spritsail; in general, this has been followed. The vertical of the foremast range also serves as the knighthead for the halyard of the foreyard. Each range has eight pins.

Cleats, in the modern sense, were quite rare; when the word is used it nearly always means the yardarm cleats, which have a rather different function. However, the *Treatise on Rigging* does refer to buntlines being 'belayed to two cleats set to either side of the main mast' (p 51). Following this, it is assumed that there were a few more cleats on the main mast, as there is a shortage of belaying points in that area. These would only be suitable for ropes which did not have to bear a great deal of weight.

Knightheads are mentioned in all the accounts, especially in connection with the halyards of the lower yards. The main ones have three sheaves for the halyard, and one more for the top-rope. It is assumed that the top-rope was not permanently rove, but was used only when the topmast had to be taken down, for example, in a storm. Each knighthead has its top carved in the form of a head. Apart from that of the foremast, which is combined with the range, there is one knighthead aft of the main mast, and one aft of the mizzen.

'Kevels' are fixed to the sides of the ship, on the inside. Mainwaring suggests that they are only used for the sheets and tacks, but other sources seem to imply that more were needed. Their form is unclear but, probably, there are two types: single and double. The double type, of a form later known as a 'staghorn', has two curved pieces of timber joined by a horizontal plank. The rope is turned, figure-of-eight fashion, round the heads of the two timbers. These are used for sheets and tacks. The single kevel is a straight piece of wood with a neck near its top, and probably a sheave set in it to take most of the strain of the rope; if the sheave is not used, it might be necessary to fit an eyebolt or block in the deck to take the strain.

There are no specific references to 'timberheads' at this period, though there are some references to belaying on the rails or on timbers. It is not likely that the verticals of the rail were carried up above the level of the rail, as in later years. Instead, if ropes were to be belayed to the rail, then they were turned round the rail, or the vertical, and then hitched. This method is particularly useful at the forecastle, where the rail provides an ample number of belaying points.

Often, it is necessary to put more than one rope on each point, in order to find space for them all. They have been arranged so that only ropes which would be used together share a point. There are more than enough points on the forecastle, but the spare points on the rail would perhaps be needed for anchor tackle.

The *Treatise on Rigging* suggests that the topsail lifts should be belayed in the tops. This has been followed, though it is contradicted by Mainwaring.

# ARMAMENT

## GUNNERY TECHNIQUES

In order to understand the gunnery methods of the 1600s, it is necessary to get rid of the image of Nelson's sailors firing one broadside after another in quick succession. Reloading in the early seventeenth century was still very slow, particularly on merchant ships. There is some evidence that guns were not allowed to recoil, and that a seaman would climb outside the ship, sit astride the gun barrel, and insert the powder and shot. To do this, the ship had to break off the action after all her guns had been fired, and then retreat to reload, and this is certainly reflected in the naval tactics of the time. Even if the system of outboard loading was not used, there is conclusive evidence that the guns were not allowed to recoil, but were run in by the crews pulling on tackles. According to William Bourne, one of the main difficulties of gunnery was that 'it is very troublesome to hale them in and lade them, especially if the ship doth heel with sail bearing' (W Bourne, *Inventions and Devices*, London 1578, p 37).

When attempting to fit the guns into the confined decks of the *Susan Constant*, it is not difficult to understand why recoil was not allowed – there is very little room for recoil, especially in the forecastle, and the slightest stretch in a breech rope would cause the gun to hit some vital component of the ship. Furthermore, there were very few men to operate the guns in normal circumstances – fourteen men for eight guns. At least half would be needed to trim the sails, steer and direct the action. Probably, a merchant ship would rely on discharging its guns as a deterrent, without any real hope of reloading during the fight. The guns were not aimed but the ship was steered so that one gun would be brought to bear in turn. 'The principal thing in a gunner at sea is to be a good helmsman, and to call to him at the helm to loof, or bear up, to have his better level . . .' (Monson's *Tracts* p 33). 'They cannot bring their piece unto the mark, except it be by the steerage' (Bourne p 38). Guns were arranged so that they would be pointing in as many directions as possible at once, so that one after another was brought to bear in turn, 'upon the least yaw of the helm some one piece or another would be brought to bear' (Boteler p 259). A battle using these tactics is graphically described in Smith's *Sea Grammar* (pp 76–9).

## TYPES OF GUNS

Eight guns, minions and falcons, have already been chosen as the armament. Lists of specifications of guns of the time have been studied (Blackmore catalogue pp 392–5), and it is difficult to find any minions of less than 7ft. For reasons of space, these minimum lengths have been chosen, and even then it is difficult enough to fit them in, particularly in the forecastle, where the space is interrupted by the bowsprit. Because the ship is narrower at the bow and stern, it is necessary to place the minions in the gunroom and forepeak, and the sakers in midships.

One way round these difficulties would be to give the ship a slightly lighter armament. However, smaller guns were not necessarily much shorter; Blackmore gives lengths of about 7ft for a falcon, and 6ft for a falconet. It was certainly possible for a ship of 120 tons to carry the heavier armament, as is shown by the ordnance returns of the 1620s; therefore this has been used.

## THE MINIONS (K1)

The design of the minions is based on a gun in the Tower of London, dated 1601 (cat no 36). It is a saker, 9ft long, but it is scaled down in its longitudinal dimensions for a gun of 7ft. The Tower gun is a bronze gun, but merchant ships of the period invariably had iron guns, which had slightly thicker metal. Therefore, 10 per cent has been added to the diameters of the gun. A minion had a bore of 3¼in, fired a ball of 3¾lb, and was 3in in diameter; the gun has been given the same thickness of metal round the bore, in proportion to the size of the bore, as in the Tower gun.

## THE FALCONS (K2)

The falcons have been designed in the same way as the minions, scaling down the dimensions of the Tower gun. The standard bore of a falcon was 2¾in, and it fired a ball of 2½lb.

## THE CARRIAGES (K3, K4, K5, K6)

The design of the gun carriages is based on three main sources: a plan of *c* 1625 in the National Maritime Museum (Photograph 5), which gives a small-scale drawing of English gun carriages, the carriages recovered from the *Vasa*, and plans and specifications of English carriages from the 1700s (*Arming and Fitting* pp 282–5). Partial dimensions of carriages of the 1580s (PRO SP 16/106, f 58) have also been used. These suggest that minion carriages should have sides and beds 3½in thick, with axletrees and trucks 4in thick; all the plank of a falcon carriage is 3in thick. The height of the carriage is determined by placing the gun in the centre of the gunport. The lengths are obtained by scaling up the dimensions of the carriages in the plan of *c* 1625. The widths are largely inspired by the carriages of the *Vasa*, though it is quite easy to establish them from first principles – the side pieces, or brackets, have to be kept a little distance from the side of the gun, and the wheels or trucks have to be kept a little way out from that.

The capsquare holds the trunnions of the gun in place. There are two ringbolts or eyebolts on each side of the carriage, to hold the breech tackle or the gun tackle. Possibly, the breech tackle was passed through the aftermost eye to lead it to the side; on the other hand, it is possible that this eye was used when the gun tackles were hauling the gun in.

The trucks are held in place by linchpins passed through holes in the axles.

## GUN TACKLE (K7, K8, K9, K10)

Each gun has three ropes attached to it – the breech tackle and two gun tackles. The breech tackle is relatively thick. Its centre is attached to the cascable at the rear of the gun by opening up the strands of rope and then seizing it on each side. The ends are fixed to ringbolts in the ships side, beside the port. In later years, eyesplices were used for this, but that seems unlikely if, as Mainwaring implies, the breeching ropes were only fitted at certain times. He states (p 110) that the breech tackle was not used in fighting, but to restrain the gun in heavy seas. It should therefore be long enough to allow the gun to be run back and let the gunport close, but no longer. It would probably be fixed to the ringbolt by means of two half hitches on one end, and perhaps a bowline on the other.

The gun tackle is of much thinner rope. One end is attached to a single block. The rope is run through one sheave of a double block, back through the sheave of the single block, and then through the double block again. Each block is fitted with a hook. The one attached to the single block goes into the ringbolt in the carriage, while the one on the double block goes to an eyebolt in the side of the ship. According to Mainwaring (p 242), the 'gunners tackles' were used to 'haul in and out the ordnance'. Some of his imitators seem to imply that this means actually lifting the guns in and out during a refit or a docking, but Mainwaring is perfectly clear about it (p 108): 'Bowse, or to bowse, is a word they use when they would have men pull together, and this is chiefly used by the gunners when they haul upon their tackles to thrust a piece out at a port.' He also implies that the tackles could give some kind of traversing movement (p 109), 'when there is occasion to pull more upon one tackle than the other'.

Mainwaring has some scattered remarks on gun tackles, and these can be pieced together to confirm that they were substantially the same as those used in later years. A double block was part of the system: 'Note that double blocks do purchase more than single blocks, and therefore in all places where we have occasion to use strength with few hands we have double blocks, as to the tackle of our ordnance' (p 100). Ringbolts are 'the chief things whereunto we fasten the tackles and breechings of the great ordnance' (p 104).

If the gun was not allowed to recoil, it must be presumed that the tackles could be led inboard to haul the gun in for loading. According to the list of stores carried by Drake's fleet in 1596 (K R Andrews (ed) *The Last Voyage of Drake and Hawkins*, Hakluyt Society, 1972, p 74), there was approximately one pair of 'bowsing tackles' for every 'britching ready cut', so there is no question of having a separate tackle from the rear of the carriage. However, it is not clear what the tackles could be attached to when running the gun in, as the *Vasa* had no eyebolts or ringbolts in suitable positions. Possibly, they could be attached to the gun on the opposite side.

In heavy weather the breech tackles and the gun tackles would be lashed together, just forward of the carriage, by means of a rope called a lashing, so that the whole system would be held tight. The guns could also be secured by means of wedges nailed to the deck: 'In very foul weather also at sea, the practice is to fasten a coin [wedge] or the like piece unto a deck with these nails, to keep them close and firm unto the ships sides, lest otherwise they should chance to break loose when the ship rolls . . . and this is called the spiking up of the ordnance.' (Boteler p 224).

## THE GUNPORTS (K11, K12, K13)

A gunport lid is made up of six basic timbers: three on the outside running fore and aft and roughly following the line of the planking, and three more running up and down on the inside. Both sets of timbers are 2in thick, though part of the outer ones had to be trimmed down so that the lid fairs in with the planking.

The port lid has two hinges, which are modelled on those shown in a plan of *c* 1625. A ringbolt is fitted to the lower centre on the outside. This serves to hold one end of the port tackle, which is taken through a hole in the side of the ship above the gunport, and is used to raise the lid. The port tackle is linked to a block and tackle arrangement inside the hull, and its inner end is attached to one of the beams or ledges of the upper deck.

The gunport also has two ringbolts inside. These are used to bar the port shut in heavy weather.

## MAGAZINES

There is no reason to believe that any special structure was made to store the powder. It would certainly be kept below the waterline, and in a secure compartment. In practice, this means the store rooms forward. In normal circumstances, a small merchant ship would carry only a few barrels, as she would not expect to fire many rounds, since the rate of fire was very slow. But, of course, the *Susan Constant* would have carried somewhat more, for the use of the colonists.

Again, a merchant ship would not normally carry much shot – perhaps five or six rounds per gun. There is no evidence that it was placed in racks round the deck, as in the eighteenth century. Indeed, a late seventeenth-century drawing shows shot stacked and placed under a tarpaulin, in action. Mainwaring (p 181) mentions that lockers could be used for storing shot, but it seems likely that these were mainly used on warships. When not in action, it could be stored almost anywhere, perhaps in the store rooms along with the powder.

# The Photographs

**1** One of the Matthew Baker draughts, showing a relatively low-built ship of around 200 tons.

*Magdalene College, Cambridge*

**2** The head of the *Prince Royal* of 1610, from a painting by Vroom.

*The Science Museum*

**3** Another ship in the same painting, the *Red Lion* of 1609, with a lion figurehead.

*Frans Halsmuseum*

**4** A rather primitive model in the Ashmolean Museum, Oxford. This is possibly the earliest English ship model, and is believed to date from around 1630. It is not known if it represents a particular ship, and it is certainly not to scale.

*Ashmolean Museum*

**5** A plan in the National Maritime Museum of around 1625. It gives some details of contemporary decorations, and a useful cross-section of the ship. Oars would only be used on a fast-sailing warship, and not on a merchantman like the *Susan Constant*.

*National Maritime Museum*

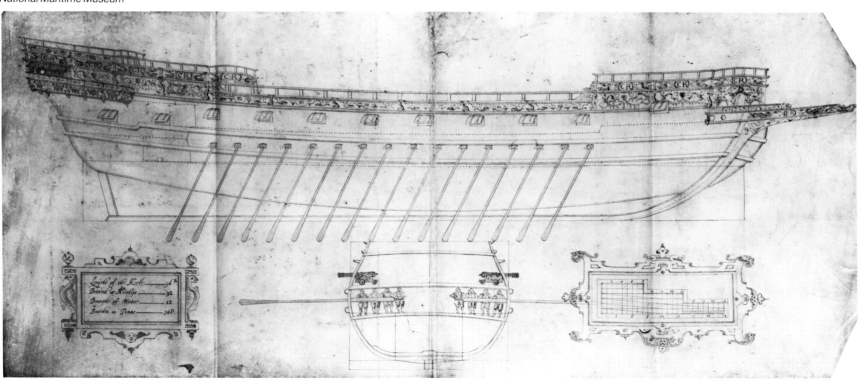

43

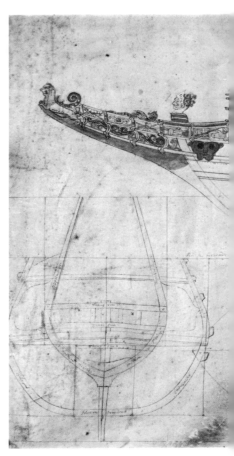

**6** Another of the Matthew Baker draughts, showing the common system of decoration around 1586.

*The Science Museum*

**7** A draught in the Riksarkivet, Copenhagen, of English origin. It is probably contemporary with the plan of 1625 in the National Maritime Museum (Photograph 5), and also gives some detail of decoration.

*Riksarkivet*

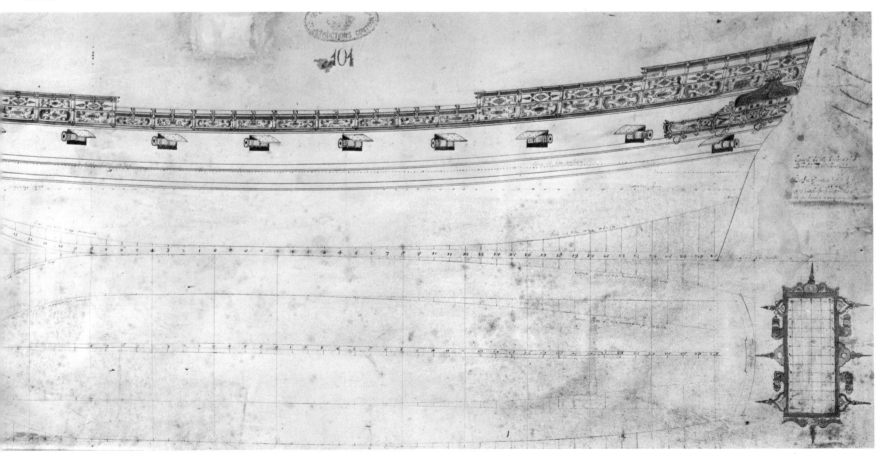

**8** Small merchant ships from John Speed's map of Cornwall, 1610.

*Author's collection*

**9** Another ship from the Vroom painting, the *Repulse* of 1610. It shows a Dutch-type tiller fitting, though this may be inaccurate; Dutch artists often imagined Dutch features on English ships.

*Frans Halsmuseum*

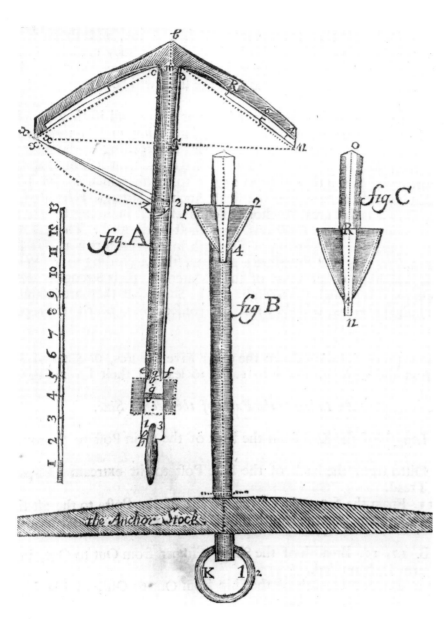

**10** The anchor from Sutherland's *Shipbuilding Unveiled*.
*National Maritime Museum*

**11** Visscher's print of the *White Bear*, one of the ships which fought the Spanish Armada in 1588. It shows some details of fitting, including a cathead which appears to lead forward from the bow.
*National Maritime Museum*

The Tower

Tower Warf

**12** Visscher's print of London in 1610 shows many interesting small merchant ships off the Tower of London. Again, there is a risk that Dutch features might be shown by mistake, though most of the ships quite plainly fly the English flag.

*Author's collection*

**13** Part of a map of Virginia in De Bry's *America*. It shows the kind of small ships which took part in Raleigh's expedition.

*British Library*

**14** English ships, mostly hired merchantmen, on an expedition to the Île de Rè in 1627. This shows the high stern which was common at that time.

*National Maritime Museum*

**15** An English ship, the *Defiance*, depicted by Vroom in the 1580s.

*National Maritime Museum*

**16** The arrival of the Elector Palatine off Margate in 1613, showing some details of the *Prince Royal* and other warships.

*National Maritime Museum*

**17** The English ship *Griffin* in the Armada campaign, drawn by Visscher.

*National Maritime Museum*

**18** An English ship (centre) engaged by a Spanish galley, *c* 1603.

*National Maritime Museum*

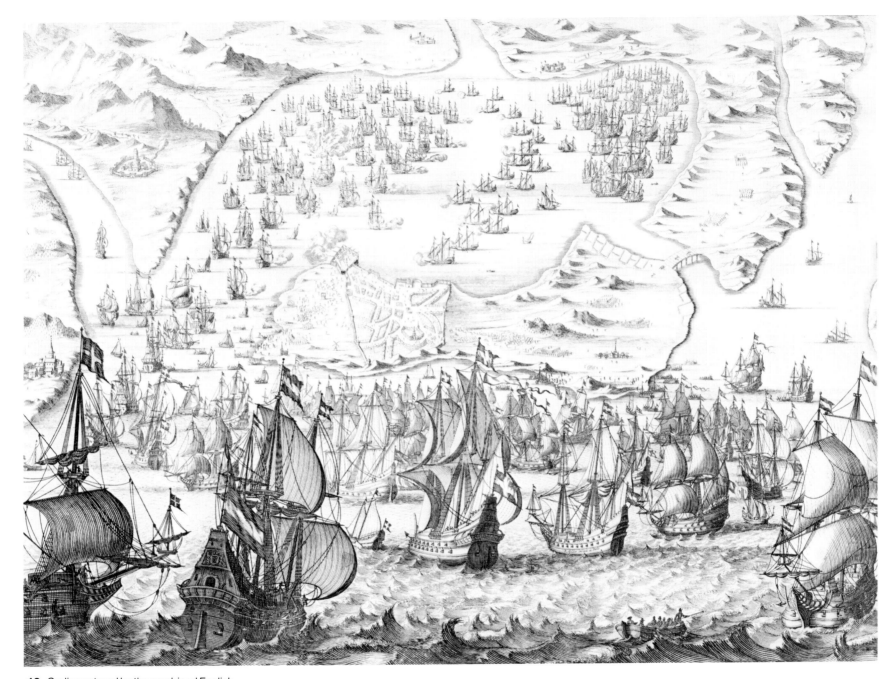

**19** Cadiz captured by the combined English and Dutch fleets in 1596, showing several English ships (with the crosses on their flags).

*National Maritime Museum*

# The Drawings

# A General layout

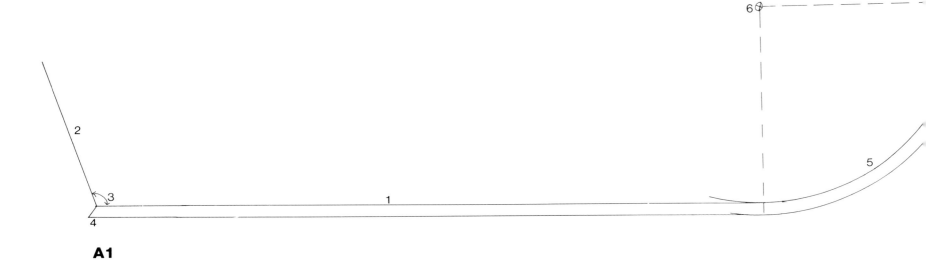

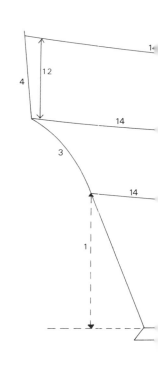

**A1**

**A2    PRINCIPLES OF DECK HEIGHT
(1/96 scale)**

**1**    Height of sternpost (equal to height of
deck in bows)
**2**    Height of deck in bows
**3**    Counter of stern
**4**    Flat of the stern
**5**    Vertical part of the stempost
**6**    Height of the breadth at the midship
frame
**7**    Thickness of deck beam
**8**    Height of the deck in midships
**9**    Camber of the decks
**10**    Rises of the deck
**11**    Height between decks – 6ft
**12**    Height at the stern – 7ft
**13**    Height of the forecastle – 5ft 9in
**14**    Line of the deck at the sides

**A2**

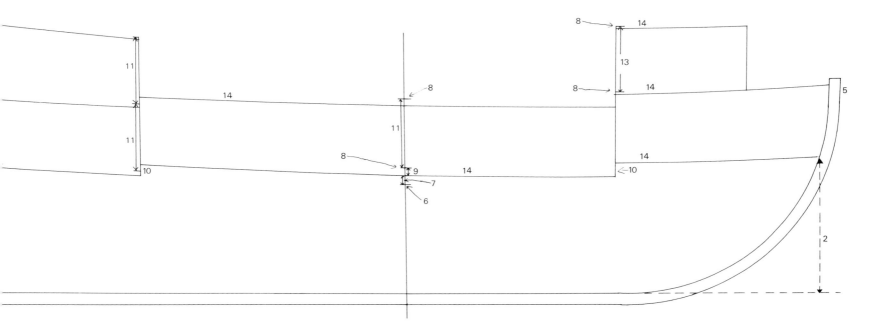

# A   General layout

**A3**

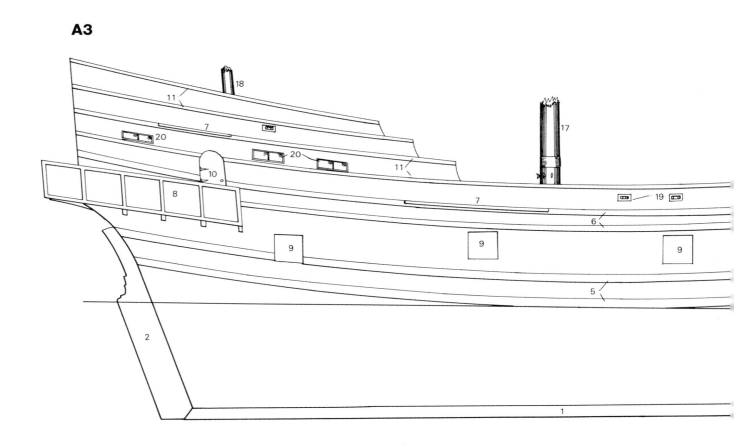

**A3** **OUTBOARD PROFILE**
**(1/96 scale)**
1 Keel
2 Rudder
3 Stempost
4 Knee of the head
5 Main wales
6 Channel wales
7 Channels
8 Gallery
9 Gunports
10 Door to gallery
11 Rails
12 Head
13 Figurehead
14 Bowsprit
15 Cathead
16 Foremast
17 Mainmast
18 Mizzenmast
19 Sheaves
20 Lights

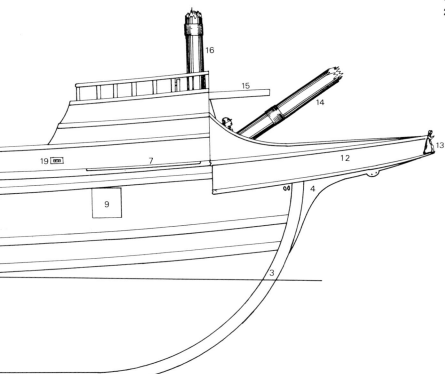

**A4**

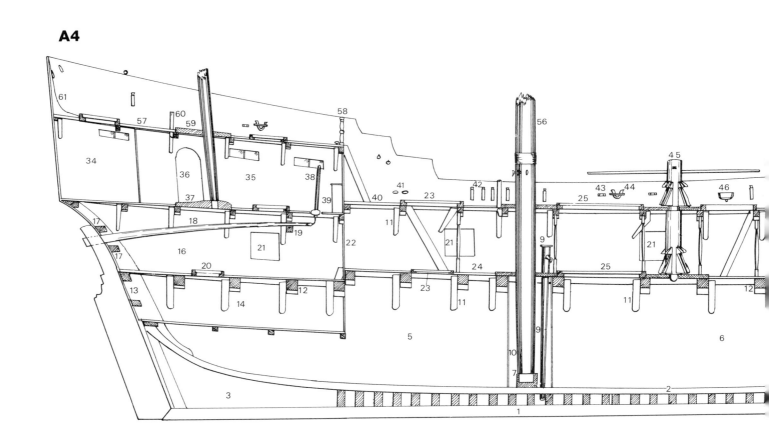

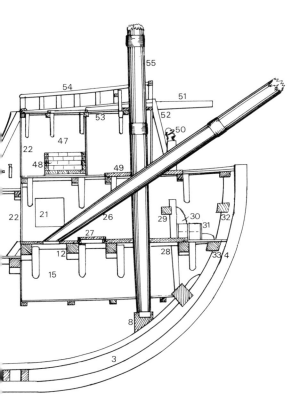

| **A4** | **INBOARD PROFILE** |
|---|---|
| | **(1/96 scale)** |
| **1** | Keel |
| **2** | Kelson |
| **3** | Deadwood |
| **4** | False stempost |
| **5** | After hold |
| **6** | Fore hold |
| **7** | Mainmast step |
| **8** | Foremast step |
| **9** | Pump |
| **10** | Pump well |
| **11** | Hanging knees |
| **12** | Deck beams |
| **13** | Stemson knee |
| **14** | Bread room |
| **15** | Store rooms in bows |
| **16** | Gunroom |
| **17** | Transoms |
| **18** | Tiller |
| **19** | Support for tiller |
| **20** | Hatch to bread room |
| **21** | Gunports |
| **22** | Bulkhead |
| **23** | After hatch |
| **24** | Lower deck |
| **25** | Main hatch |
| **26** | Fore peak |
| **27** | Scuttle to store room |
| **28** | Main bitts |
| **29** | Crosspiece |
| **30** | Knee |
| **31** | Manger |
| **32** | Breast hook |
| **33** | Deck hook |
| **34** | Great cabin |
| **35** | Steerage |
| **36** | Door to gallery |
| **37** | Mizzenmast step |
| **38** | Whipstaff |
| **39** | Binnacle |
| **40** | Upper deck |
| **41** | Cleats |
| **42** | Kevels |
| **43** | Sheave |
| **44** | Kevel |
| **45** | Capstan |
| **46** | Piss-dale |
| **47** | Cook room |
| **48** | Furnace |
| **49** | Foremast partners |
| **50** | Knighthead |
| **51** | Cathead |
| **52** | Ladder |
| **53** | Forecastle deck |
| **54** | Forecastle rail |
| **55** | Foremast |
| **56** | Mainmast |
| **57** | Quarterdeck |
| **58** | Quarterdeck rail |
| **59** | Mizzenmast partners |
| **60** | Knighthead |
| **61** | Taffrail knee |

# A  General layout

**A5  ARRANGEMENTS OF FRAMES AT GUNPORTS (1/48 scale)**
1  Port cill
2  Thickness of frame, 5in
3  'Room and space', 1ft 7in
4  Height and breadth of port, 2ft 3in

**A5**

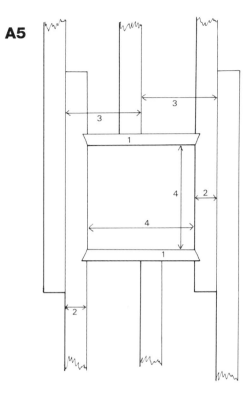

**A6**

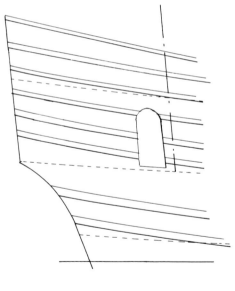

**A6  DETAILS OF WALES, ETC, UNDER BEAKHEAD AND STERN GALLERY (1/46 scale)**

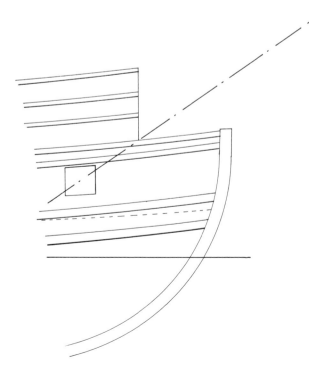

# B Hull form

**B1** **Details Of Midship Frame**
**(1/48 scale)**
**1** Keel
**2** Floor
**3** Centre of floor sweep
**4** Floor sweep
**5** Centre of breadth sweep
**6** Breadth sweep
**7** Centre of reconciling sweep
**8** Reconciling sweep
**9** To centre of toptimber sweep
**10** Toptimber sweep
**11** Toptimber line

## B1

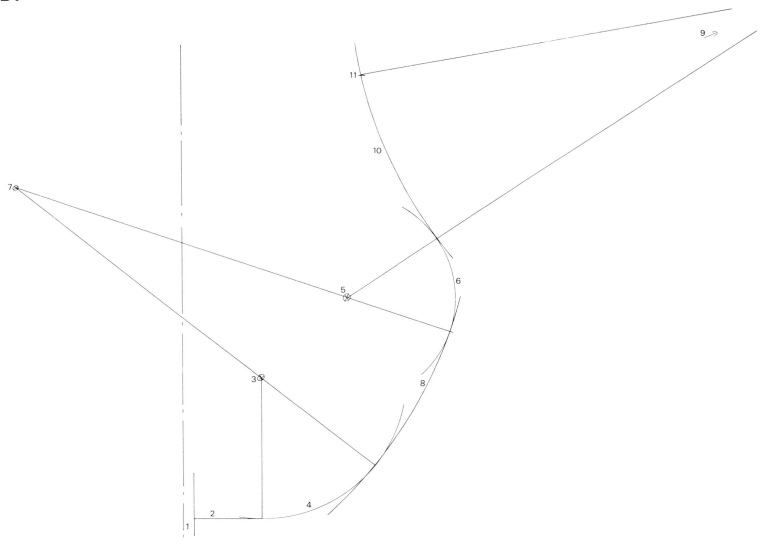

# B Hull form

**B2**

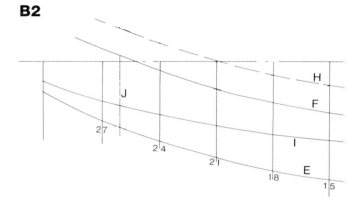

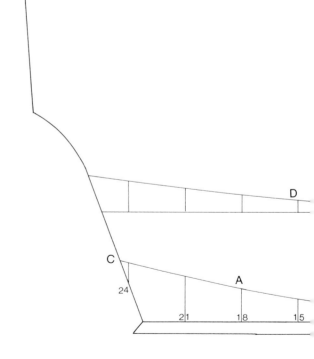

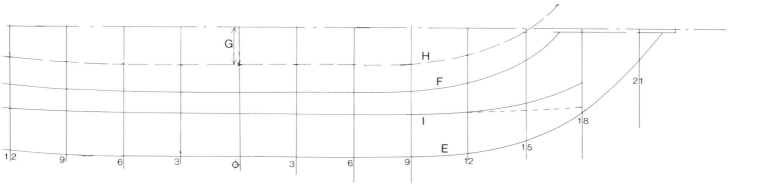

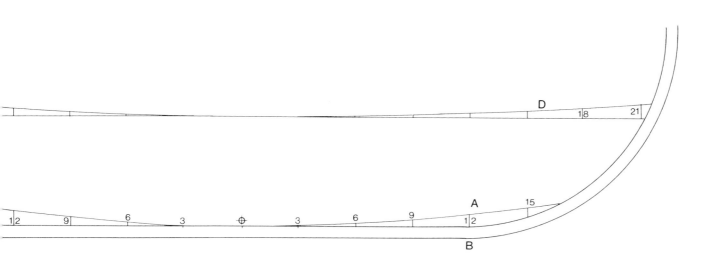

**B3**  **FRAME 21 AFT**
 **(1/48 scale)**

 1  Centre of floor sweep
 2  Floor sweep
 3  Centre of reconciling sweep
 4  Reconciling sweep
 5  Centre of breadth sweep
 6  Breadth sweep
 7  To centre of toptimber sweep
 8  Toptimber sweep
 9  Toptimber line
10  Gunwale
11  Keel
12  Centre of dead rising curve
13  Reverse curve of dead rising

**B3**

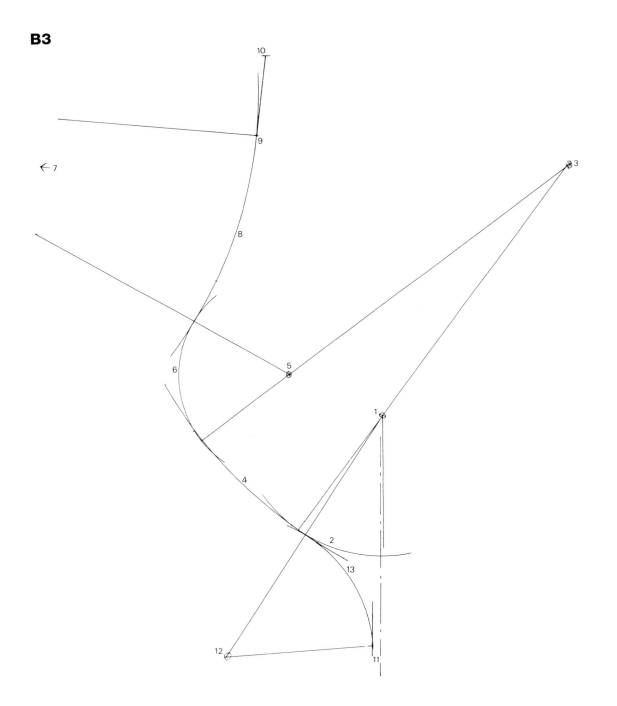

**B4** **LINES PLAN SHOWING DIAMETERS
OF FLOOR AND BREADTH SWEEP
(1/48 scale)**
**A** Breadth sweeps
**B** Floor sweeps

**B4**

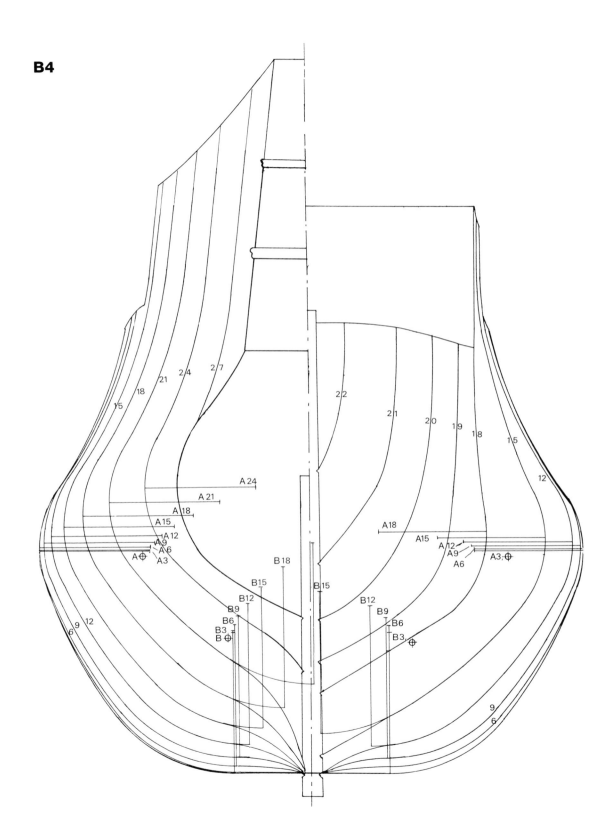

65

**B5**

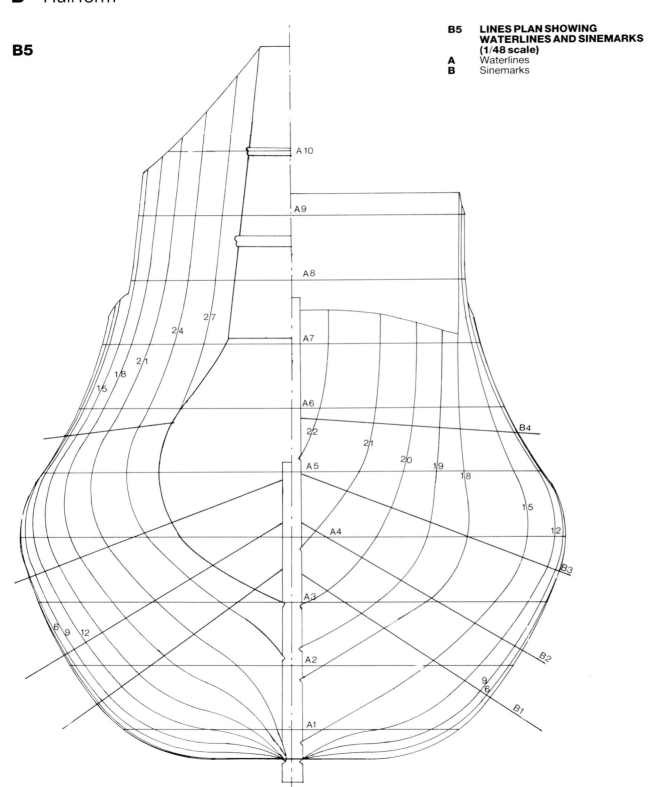

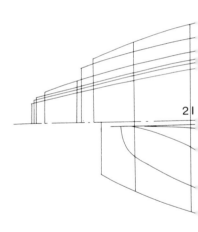

**B6**

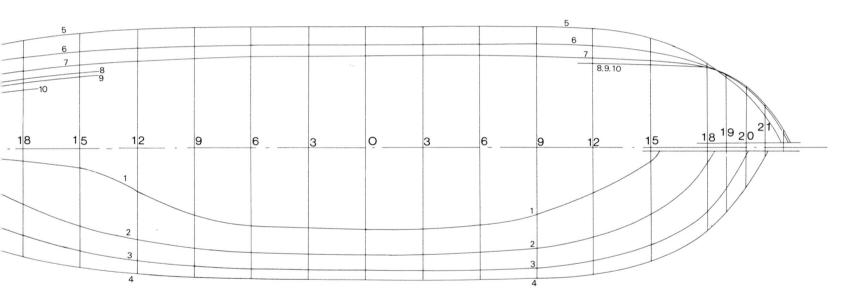

# C Structure

C1

**C2**

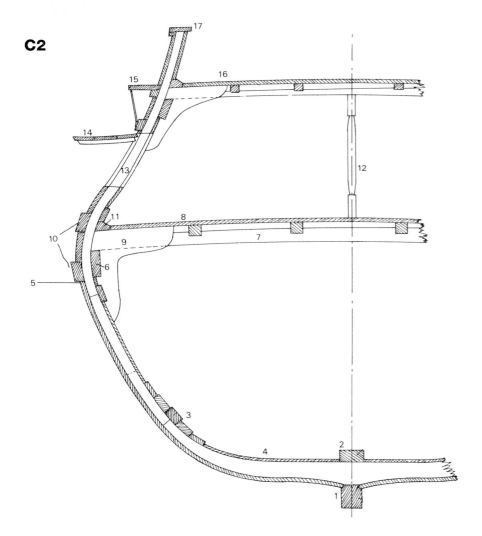

# C  Structure

**C3**

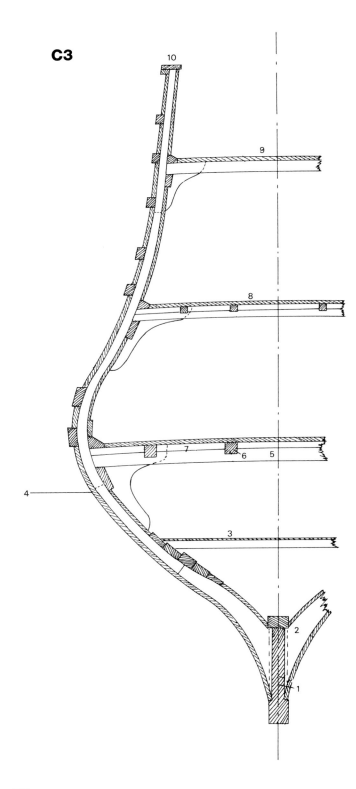

**C4**

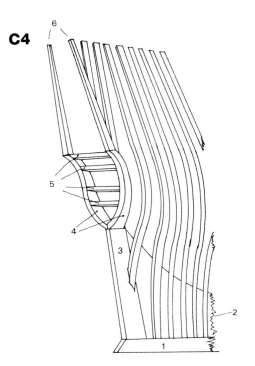

**C4  STRUCTURE OF THE STERN**
**(no scale)**
1  Keel
2  Deadwood
3  Sternpost
4  Fashion pieces
5  Transoms
6  Stern timbers

**C3  SECTION AT FRAME 21 AFT**
**(1/48 scale)**
1  Deadwood
2  Half frame
3  Bread room platform
4  Waterline
5  Lower deck beam
6  Carline
7  Ledge
8  Upper deck
9  Quarterdeck
10  Rail

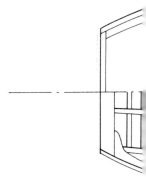

**C5 LOWER DECK**
**(1/96 scale)**
1 Gunports
2 Hatch to bread room
3 After hatch (ladder above)
4 Partners of mainmast
5 Mainmast
6 Pump
7 Main hatch
8 Waterway
9 Capstan
10 Capstan partners
11 Hawse holes
12 Position of bowsprit partners
13 Hatch to store rooms
14 Partners of foremast
15 Foremast
16 Bitt pin
17 Crosspiece of bitts
18 Knee
19 Hanging knees
20 Lodging knees
21 Carlines
22 Ledges
23 Deck beams

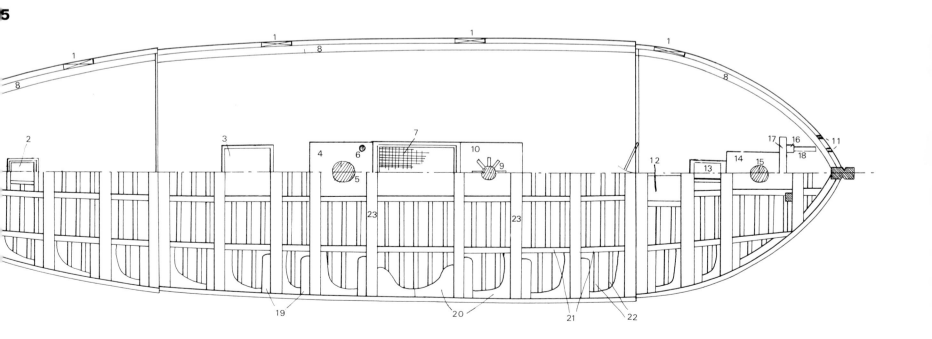

# C  Structure

**C6**

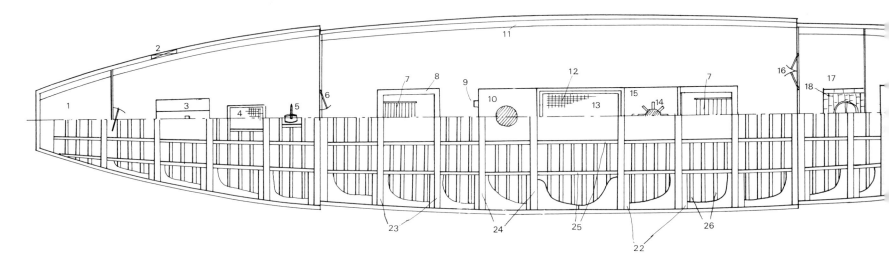

**C7**

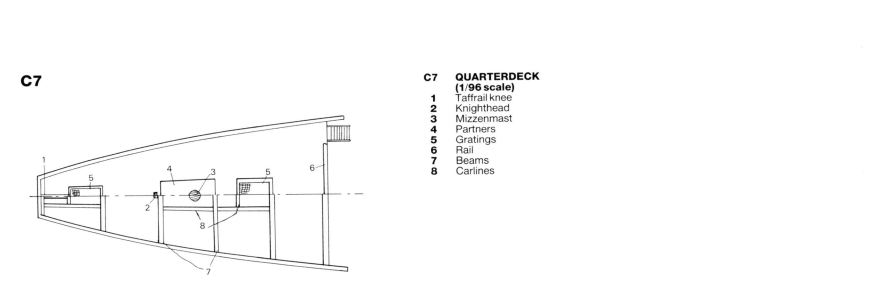

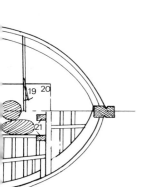

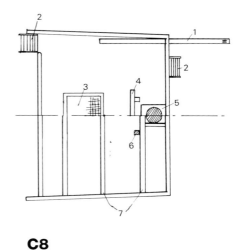

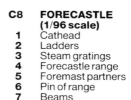

**C8  FORECASTLE**
**(1/96 scale)**
1   Cathead
2   Ladders
3   Steam gratings
4   Forecastle range
5   Foremast partners
6   Pin of range
7   Beams

**C8**

**C9  STORE ROOM IN BOW**
**(1/96 scale)**
1   Bulkhead
2   Beams
3   Foremast

**C10  BREAD ROOM**
**(1/96 scale)**
1   Beams
2   Bulkhead

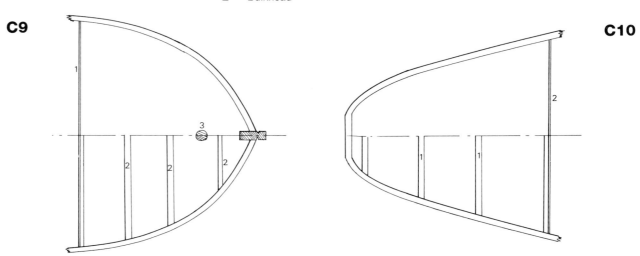

**C9**

**C10**

# D Decoration

**D1**

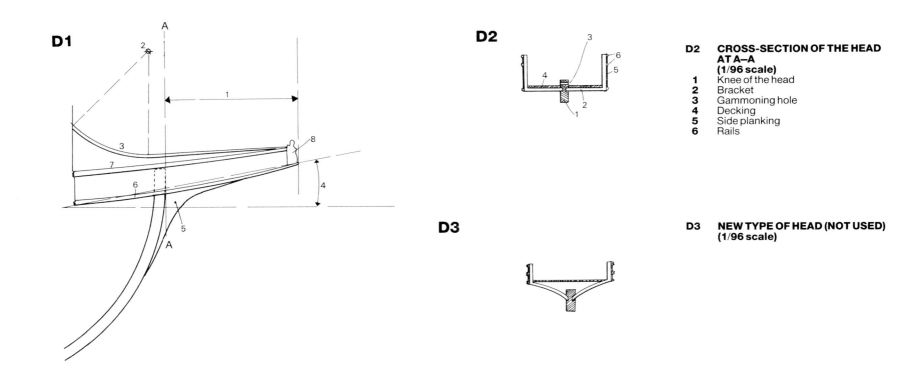

**D2**

**D3**

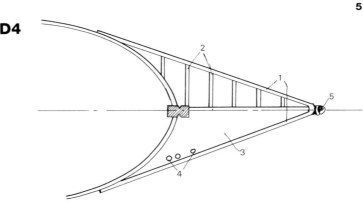

**D1**  **PROFILE OF THE HEAD**
**(1/96 scale)**
1  Length of the head – 1/5 of the keel
2  Centre of the sweep of the hancing
piece
3  Hancing piece – diameter 8ft 11in
4  Steeving, 12 degrees
5  Knee of the head
6  Lower rail
7  Upper rail
8  Figurehead

**D2**  **CROSS-SECTION OF THE HEAD**
**AT A—A**
**(1/96 scale)**
1  Knee of the head
2  Bracket
3  Gammoning hole
4  Decking
5  Side planking
6  Rails

**D3**  **NEW TYPE OF HEAD (NOT USED)**
**(1/96 scale)**

**D4**  **PLAN OF THE HEAD**
**(1/96 scale)**
1  Sides
2  Brackets
3  Planking
4  Holes for toilet
5  Figurehead

**D5**

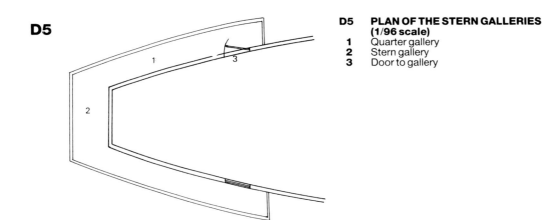

**D5    PLAN OF THE STERN GALLERIES**
**(1/96 scale)**
**1**    Quarter gallery
**2**    Stern gallery
**3**    Door to gallery

**D6**

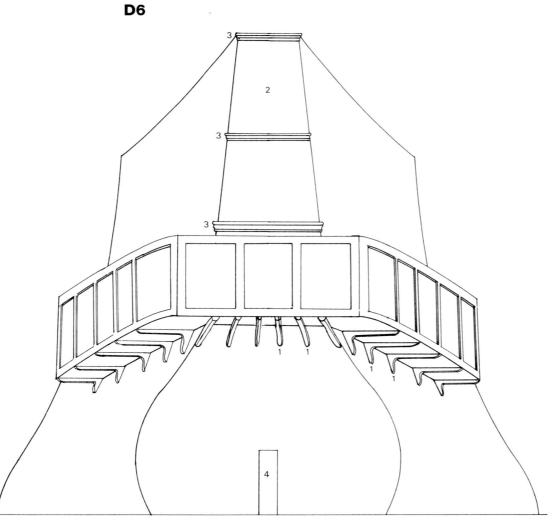

**D6    STERN, SHOWING GALLERIES**
**(1/96 scale)**
**1**    Brackets
**2**    Flat of the stern
**3**    Rails
**4**    Sternpost

75

# E Fittings

**E1  RUDDER**
**(1/48 scale)**
1  Skeg
2  Pintle
3  Gudgeon
4  Sternpost
5  Hancing
6  Tiller
7  Tenon
8  Rear view
9  Section at A–A
10  Section at B–B
11  Counter

**E2  DETAILS OF STEERING SYSTEM**
**(no scale)**
1  Pintle
2  Gudgeon
3  Whipstaff
4  Tiller
5  Gooseneck

**E2**

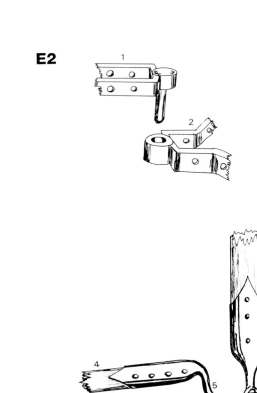

**E1**

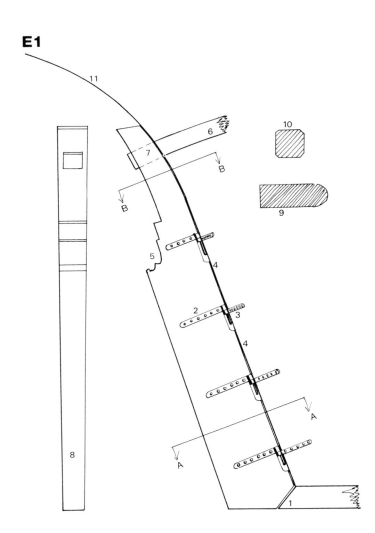

**E3**

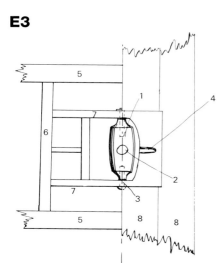

**E4**

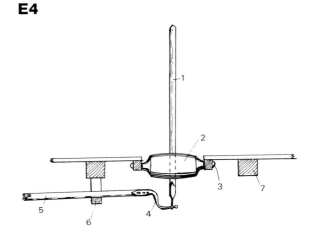

**E3    TOP VIEW OF WHIPSTAFF ROWLE**
**(1/24 scale)**

1    Rowle
2    Hole for whipstaff
3    Bolt
4    Groove for whipstaff in extreme position
5    Deck beam
6    Carline
7    Ledges
8    Deck planking

**E4    SIDE VIEW OF WHIPSTAFF MOUNTING**
**(1/24 scale)**

1    Whipstaff
2    Rowle
3    Bolt
4    Gooseneck
5    Tiller
6    Support for tiller
7    Deck beam

**E5    WHIPSTAFF IN NEUTRAL POSITION**
**(1/24 scale)**

1    Whipstaff
2    Rowle
3    Bolt
4    Tiller
5    Support for tiller
6    Gooseneck
7    Deck beam
8    Carline
9    Ledge

**E6    WHIPSTAFF IN OTHER POSITIONS**
**(1/24 scale)**

1    Whipstaff at about 15-degree rudder
2    At about 10-degree rudder

**E6**

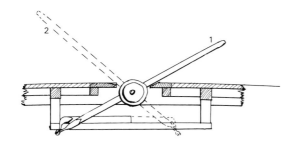

**E5**

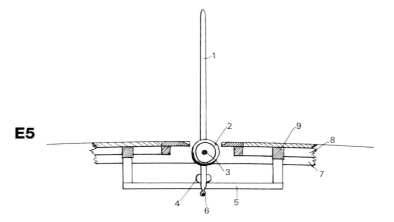

# E Fittings

**E8**

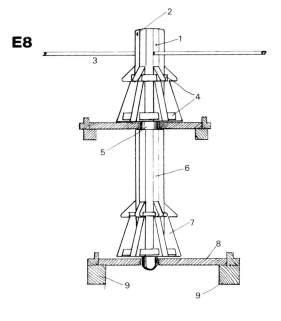

**E7**

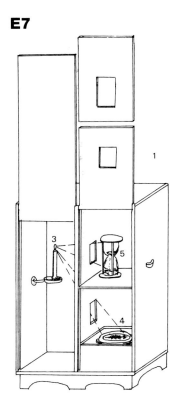

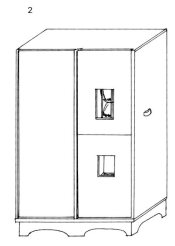

**E9**

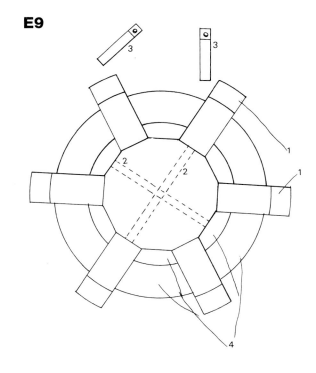

# E10

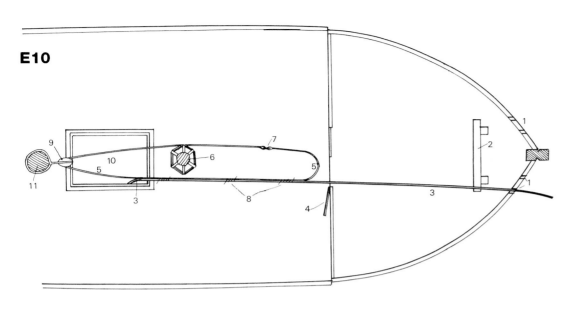

# E11

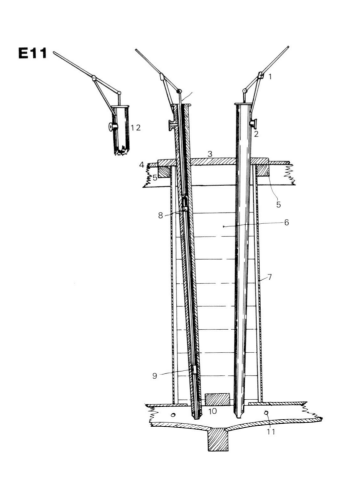

# E12

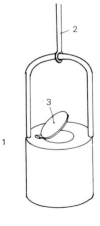

**E13**

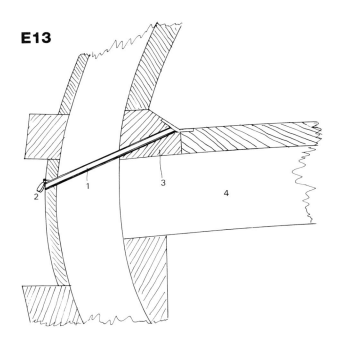

**E13  DETAILS OF SCUPPERS**
**(no scale)**
**1**  Scupper
**2**  Leather flap
**3**  Waterway
**4**  Deck beam

**E14  APPROXIMATE POSITIONS OF**
**SCUPPERS**
**(1/192 scale)**
**1**  Waterline
**2**  Steerage
**3**  Gun room
**4**  Upper deck
**5**  Lower deck
**6**  Fore deck
**7**  Fore peak
**8**  Scuppers

**E14**

**E15**

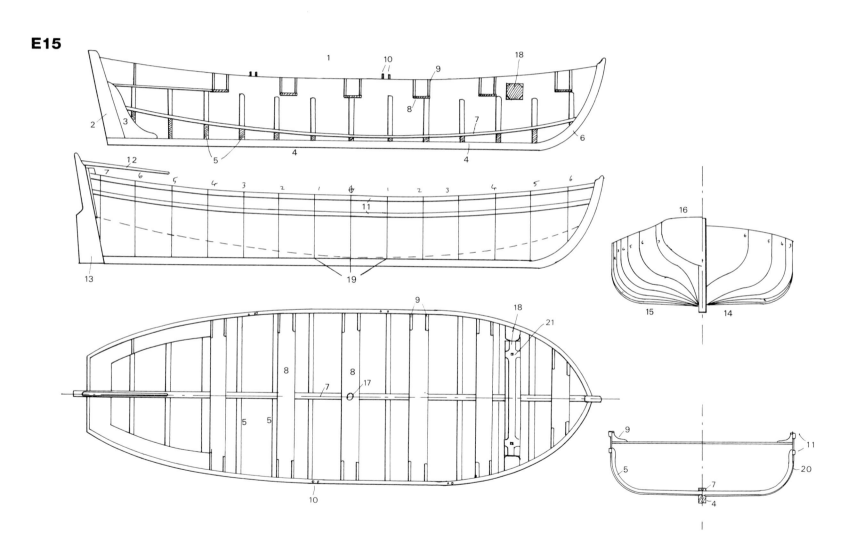

**E16** **SHALLOP**
      **(1/48 scale)**
  **1**  Longitudinal section
  **2**  Keel
  **3**  Kelson
  **4**  Thwart
  **5**  Brackets
  **6**  Thole pins
  **7**  Frame timber
  **8**  Midship section
  **9**  Wales
 **10**  Tiller
 **11**  Rudder
 **12**  Hole for mast

**E16**

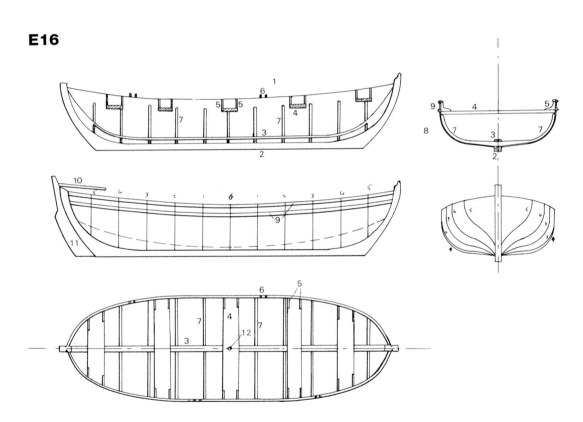

# F Accommodation

## F1

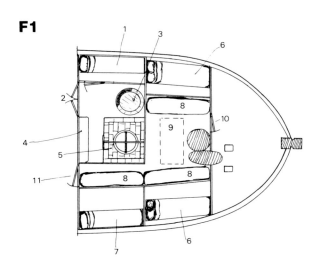

**F1 CREW'S ACCOMMODATION IN FORECASTLE**
**(1/96 scale)**

1 Cook's cabin
2 Double doors to allow entry of butt
3 Butt
4 Working table
5 Furnace
6 Cabin for two seamen
7 Boatswain's cabin
8 Seamen's palliasses
9 Table
10 Door to foredeck
11 Door to crew's cabin

**F2 ARRANGEMENT OF CABINS ON THE LOWER DECK**
**(1/96 scale)**

1 Minions
2 Falcons
3 Single cabins
4 Double cabins

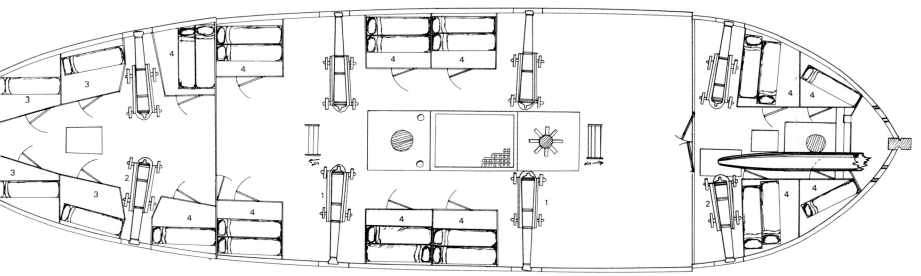

# F Accommodation

**F3**

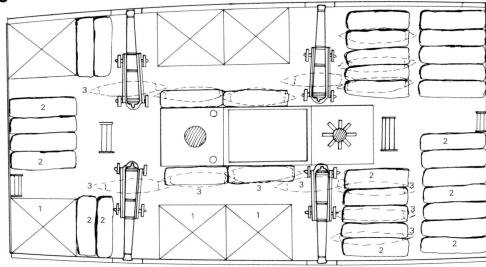

**F3** **ARRANGEMENT OF MATTRESSES AND HAMMOCKS ON THE LOWER DECK**
(1/96 scale)

1 Cabins
2 Palliasses
3 Hammocks (dotted lines)

**F4**

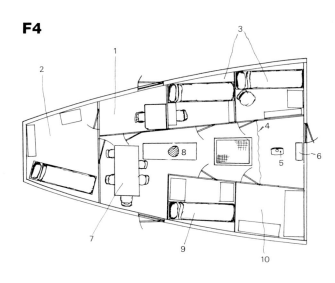

**F4** **CABINS UNDER THE QUARTERDECK**
(1/96 scale)

1 Captain's day cabin
2 Captain's sleeping cabin
3 Mates' cabins
4 Curtain
5 Whipstaff
6 Binnacle
7 Table
8 Mizzenmast
9 Carpenter's cabin
10 Chart room

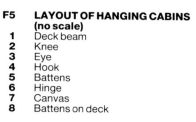

**F5**

**F5 LAYOUT OF HANGING CABINS**
**(no scale)**

1. Deck beam
2. Knee
3. Eye
4. Hook
5. Battens
6. Hinge
7. Canvas
8. Battens on deck

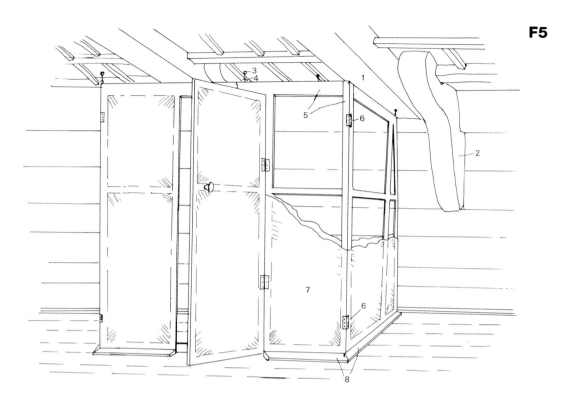

**F6**

**F6 METHOD OF FOLDING AWAY HANGING CABINS**
**(no scale)**

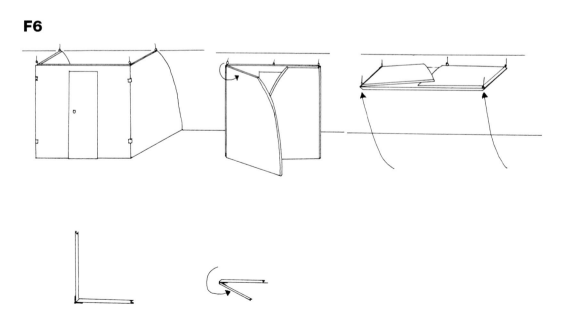

**F7**

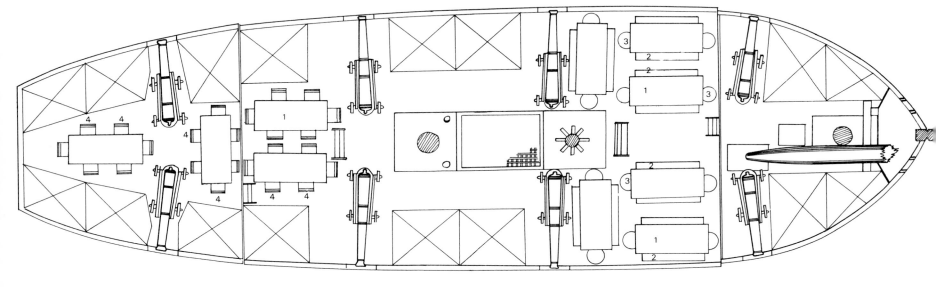

F7  **ARRANGEMENT OF TABLES ON
THE LOWER DECK
(1/96 scale)**
1  Table
2  Bench
3  Barrel seat
4  Chairs

**F8**

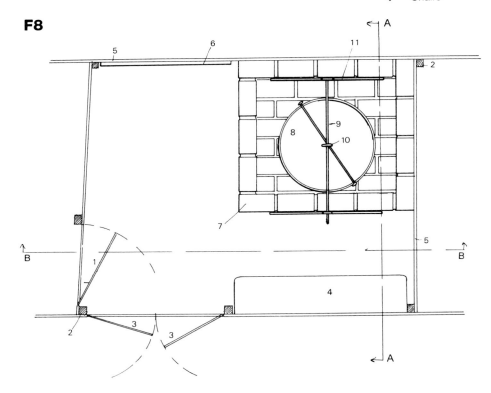

F8  **COOK ROOM, PLAN
(1/24 scale)**
1  Door to cook's cabin
2  Stanchion
3  Doors to cook room
4  Table
5  Partition
6  Hatch to seamen's quarters
7  Brickwork of furnace
8  Kettle
9  Andiron
10  Ess
11  Andiron support

**F9**

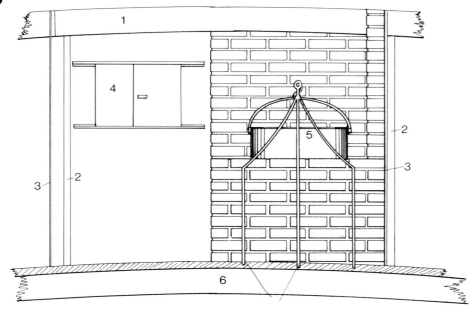

**F10**

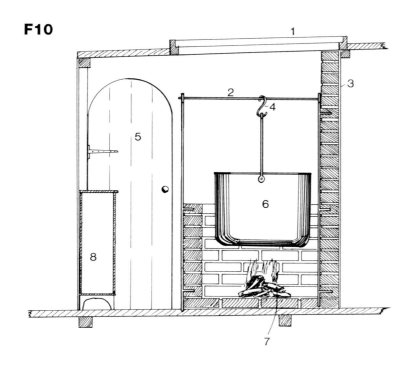

## F Accommodation

### F11

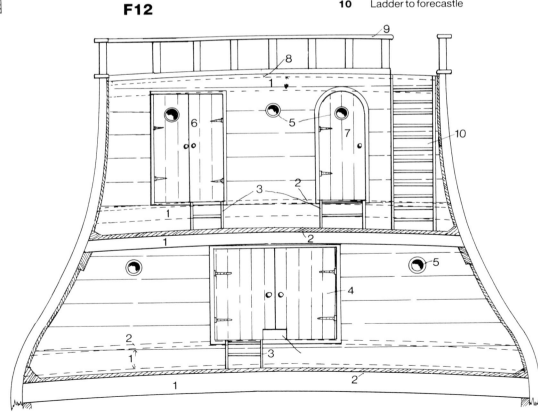

**F11** **MIDSHIP SECTION SHOWING HOLD STOWAGE (1/48 scale)**
1 Iron ballast
2 Gravel ballast
3 Ground tier
4 Second tier
5 Third tier
6 Butts
7 Wedges
8 Smaller casks to fill space round edges
9 Cables stowed on planks on casks in hold

**F12** **FORECASTLE BULKHEADS (1/48 scale)**
1 Deck beam
2 Deck plank
3 Ladder
4 Doors to fore peak
5 Loopholes
6 Doors to cookroom
7 Door to seamen's quarters
8 Forecastle deck
9 Forecastle rail
10 Ladder to forecastle

### F12

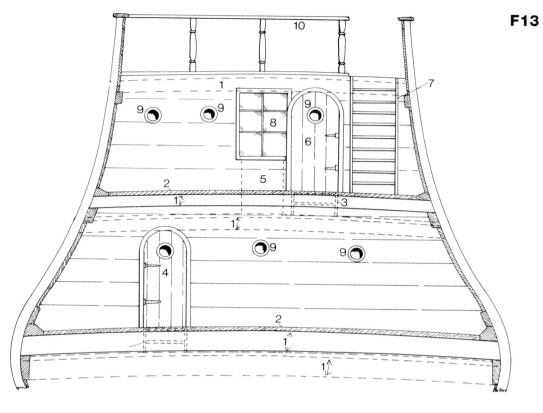

**F13**

**F13    QUARTERDECK BULKHEADS**
**(1/48 scale)**
1    Deck beam
2    Deck plank
3    Ladder
4    Door to gunroom
5    Binnacle
6    Door to cabins
7    Ladder to quarterdeck
8    Window for helmsman
9    Loopholes
10   Quarterdeck rail

**F14**

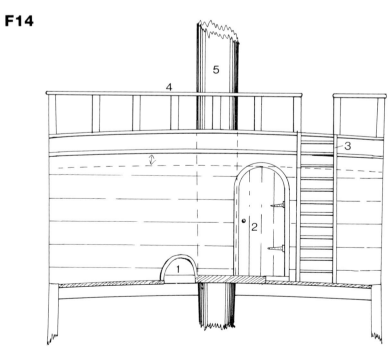

**F14    BEAKHEAD BULKHEAD**
**(1/48 scale)**
1    Hole for bowsprit
2    Door from crew's quarters
3    Ladder
4    Forecastle rail
5    Foremast

# F   Accommodation

**F15**

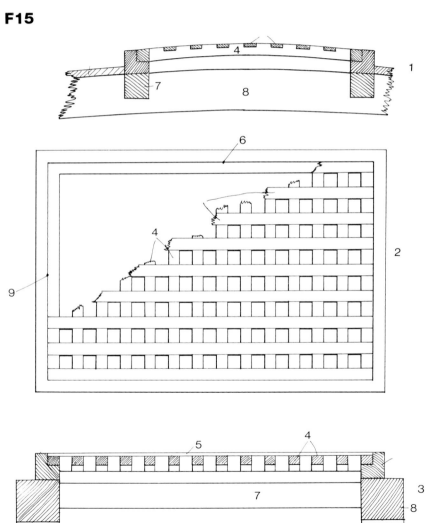

# G Masts and yards

**G1 MAINMAST**
**(1/96 scale)**
1  Heel
2  Tenon
3  Partners
4  First quarter
5  Second quarter
6  Third quarter
7  Hounds
8  Sheave
9  Head
10  Front view
11  Wolding
12  Tenon at heel (1/48 scale)

**G2 FOREMAST**
**(1/96 scale)**

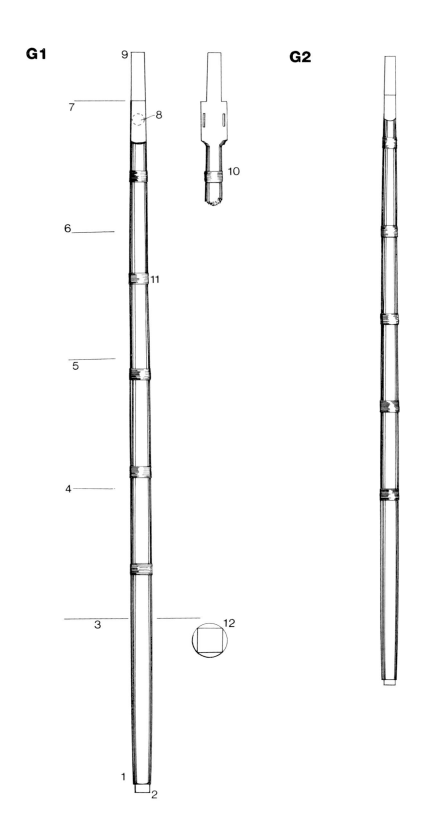

91

# G Masts and yards

**G3 DETAILS OF HOUNDS AND HEAD**
(no scale)

**G4 DETAILS OF WOLDINGS**
(1/24 scale)
1   1½in wood
2   Rope

## G3

## G4

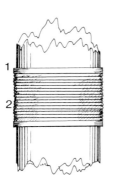

## G5

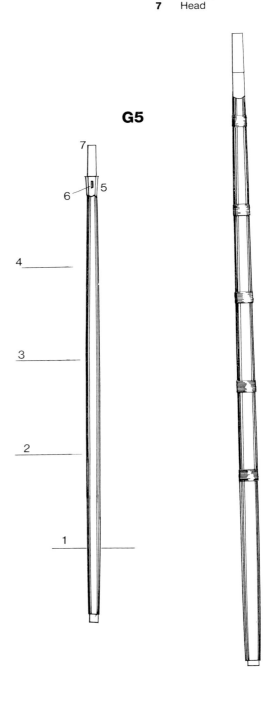

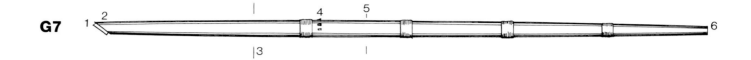

**G7**

**G6** **TOPMASTS**
**(1/96 scale)**
1  Maintopmast
2  Foretopmast
3  Position of cap
4  Heel (square)
5  Hounds (octagonal)
6  Head (square)
7  Sheave for top rope

**G7** **BOWSPRIT**
**(1/46 scale)**
1  Tenon
2  Heel
3  Partners
4  Cleats for gammoning
5  First quarter
6  Head

**G6**

**G8**

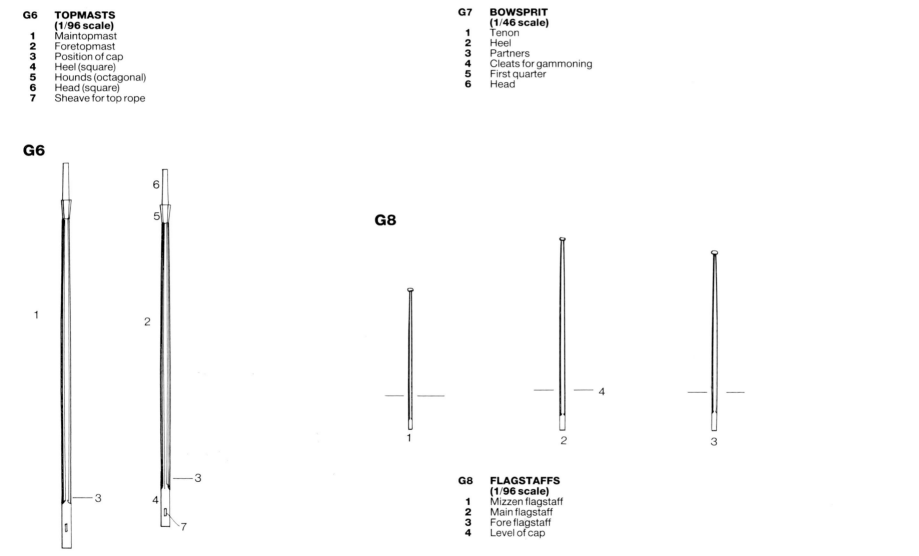

**G8** **FLAGSTAFFS**
**(1/96 scale)**
1  Mizzen flagstaff
2  Main flagstaff
3  Fore flagstaff
4  Level of cap

**G9**

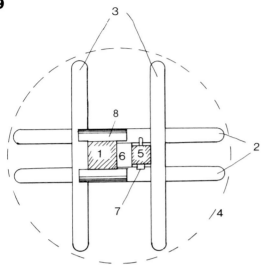

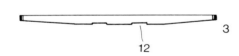

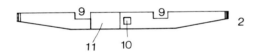

**G10 FORE TRESTLETREES**
**(1/48 scale)**
1 Foremast
2 Foretopmast

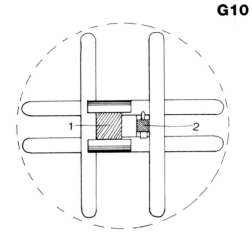

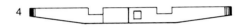

**G11**

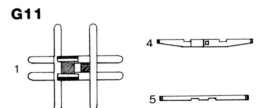

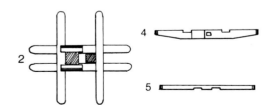

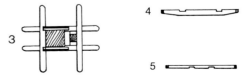

**G9 MAIN TRESTLETREES**
**(1/48 scale)**
1 Mainmast
2 Trestletrees
3 Crosstrees
4 Line of top
5 Topmast
6 Chock
7 Fid
8 Bolster
9 Recess for crosstree
10 Tenon for chock
11 Recess for lower mast
12 Recess for trestletree

**G11 SMALLER TRESTLETREES**
**(1/48 scale)**
1 Foretopmast
2 Maintopmast
3 Mizzentopmast
4 Trestletree
5 Crosstree

## G12 MAINMAST CAP
**(no scale)**

1 Distance between holes, 1ft 7½in
2 Square for mainmast head, 12in
3 Diameter of hole for topmast, 9½in
4 Length of cap, 3ft 2in
5 Breadth, 1ft 7in
6 Height, 9½in

## G13 MAIN TOP
**(1/48 scale)**

1 Plan
2 Section through centre
3 Side view
4 Lower rim
5 Upper rail
6 Lower rail
7 Knees
8 Stanchion
9 Base planking

## G12

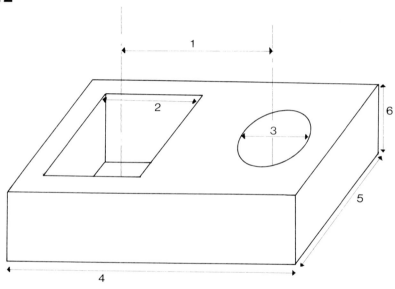

## G13

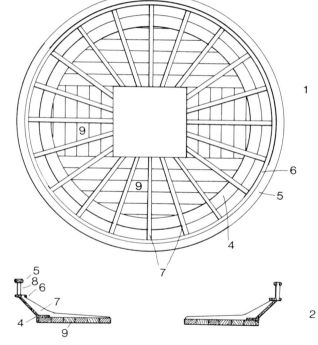

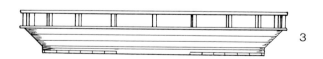

# G Masts and yards

**G14**  **FORETOP**
(1/48 scale)

**G15**  **FITTING OF TOPMAST TO**
**MAINMAST, FRONT VIEW**
(1/48 scale)
| | |
|---|---|
| **1** | Mainmast |
| **2** | Maintopmast |
| **3** | Sheave |
| **4** | Hounds |
| **5** | Trestletree |
| **6** | Crosstree |
| **7** | Top |
| **8** | Bolster |
| **9** | Cap |
| **10** | Fid |

**G14**

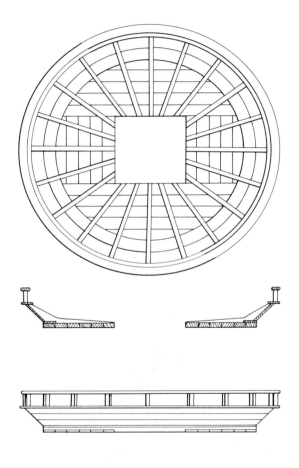

**G15**

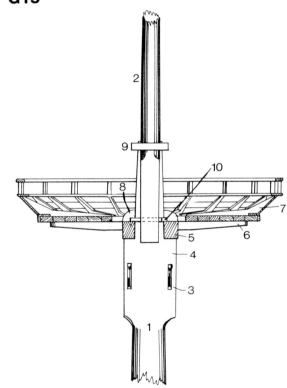

**G16   FITTING OF TOPMAST TO MAINMAST, SIDE VIEW**
**(1/48 scale)**

1 Mainmast
2 Maintopmast
3 Hounds
4 Chock
5 Trestletree
6 Crosstree
7 Fid
8 Sheave for top-rope
9 Groove for rope
10 Cap

## G16

**G17   FITTING OF FLAGSTAFF TO MAINTOPMAST**
**(1/48 scale)**

1 Main topmast
2 Trestletree
3 Cap
4 Crosstree
5 Bolster
6 Flagstaff

## G17

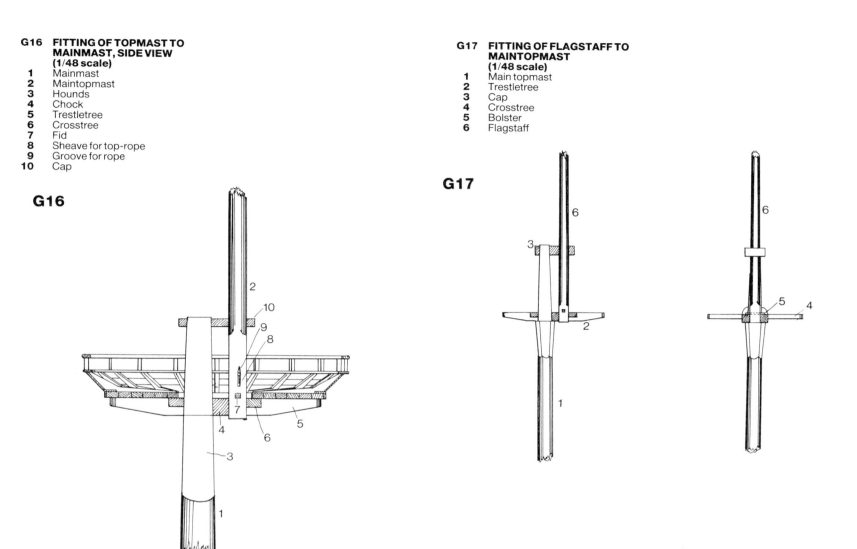

**G18   MAINYARD**
**(1/96 scale)**

1 Sling cleats
2 Robband strips
3 Yardarm cleats
4 First quarter
5 Second quarter
6 Third quarter
7 Front view
8 Plan view

## G18

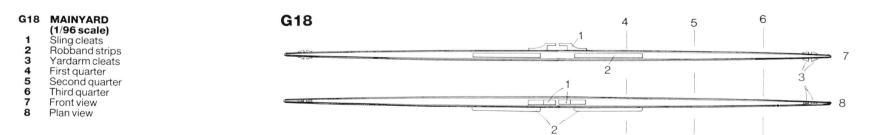

97

# G Masts and yards

**G19 DETAILS OF MAINYARD, CLEATS, ETC**
**(1/48 scale)**
1 Front view
2 Plan

**G19**

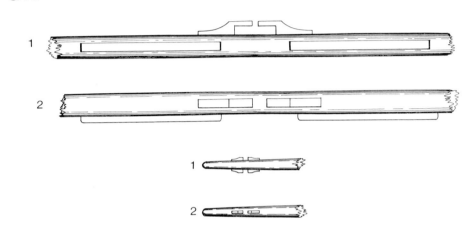

**G20**

**G20 MIZZEN YARD**
1 Plan
2 View from starboard
3 Forward

# H  Standing rigging

**H1  FITTING OF MAIN SHROUDS, ETC**
**(1/96 scale)**

1  Chains
2  Deadeyes
3  Lanyard
4  Shrouds
5  Lower catharpins
6  Pendant of tackle (one side only)
7  Futtock shrouds
8  Futtock stave
9  Upper catharpins

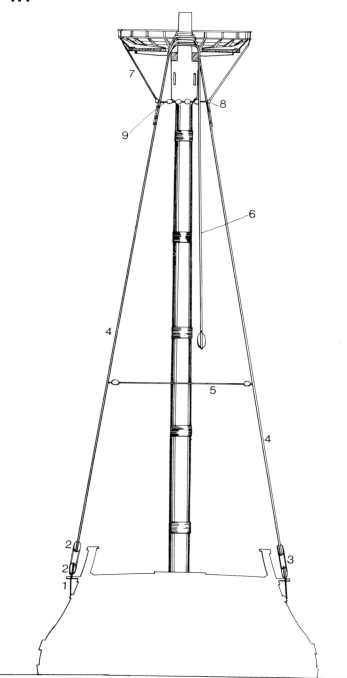

**H1**

# H Standing rigging

**H2** **SHROUDS AND STAYS**
**(1/192 scale)**
1 Foretopmast stay
2 Forestay
3 Collar
4 Mainstay
5 Maintopmast stay
6 Mizzenstay
7 Collar of main stay
8 Shrouds
9 Ratlines
10 Pendant
11 Backstay
12 Backstay pendant
13 Backstay fall

**H2**

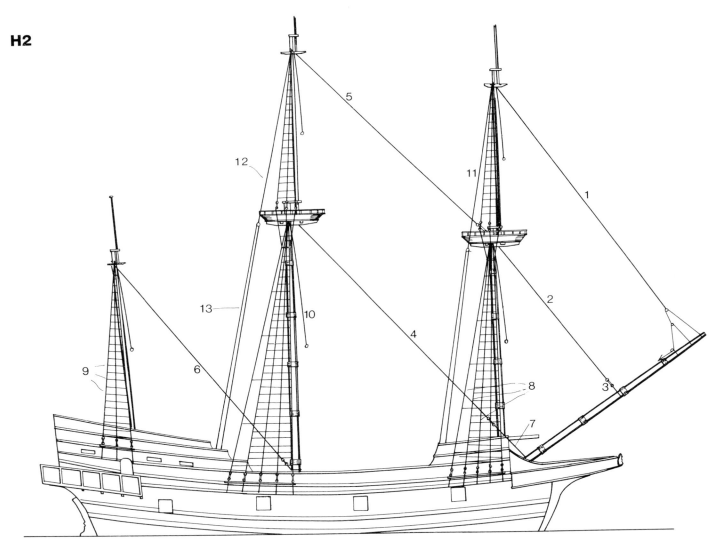

**H3     FITTING OF MAIN TOPMAST**
           **SHROUDS**
           **(1/96 scale)**

| | |
|---|---|
| 1 | Topmast shrouds |
| 2 | Deadeyes |
| 3 | Futtock shrouds |
| 4 | Futtock stave |
| 5 | Ends of futtock shrouds seized to lower shrouds |
| 6 | Pendant block (both sides) |

**H4**

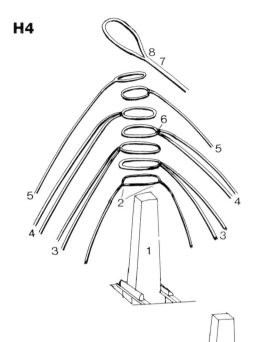

**H5     FITTING OF DEADEYES TO**
           **LOWER SHROUDS**
           **(1/24 scale)**

| | |
|---|---|
| 1 | Channel |
| 2 | Upper channel wale |
| 3 | Lower channel wale |
| 4 | Chain plate |
| 5 | Hook |
| 6 | Bolt |
| 7 | Lower deadeye |
| 8 | Upper deadeye |
| 9 | Lanyard |
| 10 | Knot |
| 11 | End of lanyard turned round shroud |
| 12 | End of lanyard seized to shroud |
| 13 | Shroud |
| 14 | Seizing |

**H3**

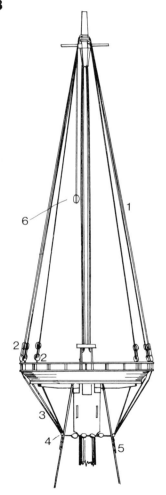

**H5**

**H4     FITTING OF SHROUDS AND STAY**
           **TO MASTHEAD**
           **(no scale)**

| | |
|---|---|
| 1 | Masthead |
| 2 | Pendant |
| 3 | First and second shrouds |
| 4 | Third and fourth shrouds |
| 5 | Fifth shroud |
| 6 | Seizing |
| 7 | Stay |
| 8 | Eyesplice |
| 9 | Shrouds |
| 10 | Bolster |

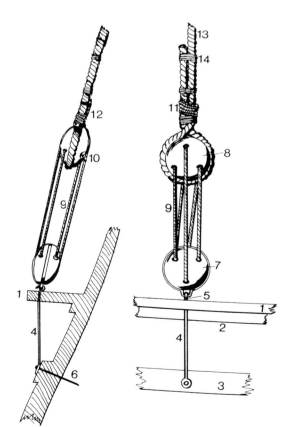

# H  Standing rigging

**H7**

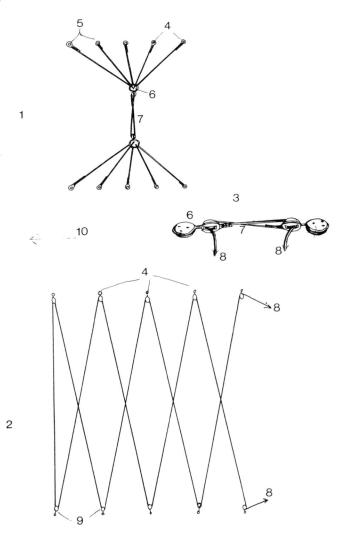

**H6**

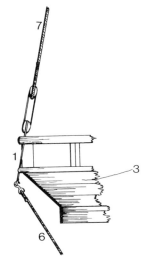

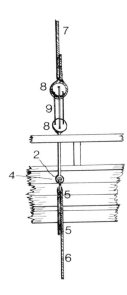

## H8 FITTING OF RATLINES
**(no scale)**
1 Shrouds
2 Swifter
3 Ratlines
4 Clove hitches

## H9 PREPARATION OF STANDING RIGGING
**(no scale)**
1 Worming
2 Parcelling
3 Serving

**H8**

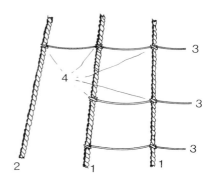

**H9**

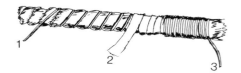

## H11 GAMMONING OF BOWSPRIT
**(1/96 scale)**
1 Stempost
2 Knee of the head
3 Beams of the head
4 Bowsprit
5 Knighthead
6 Gammon hole
7 Gammoning
8 Gammon lashing
9 Top of the knee of the head
10 Collar of main stay

## H10 TYPICAL STAY COLLAR
**(no scale)**
1 Deadeye
2 Seizing
3 Eyesplice
4 Rope for seizing eyesplices together

**H10**

**H11**

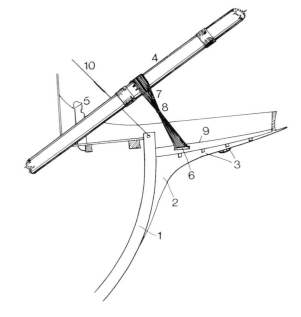

# I Sails

**I1 SAIL PLAN**
**(1/192 scale)**
1   Spritsail
2   Fore course
3   Bonnet
4   Foretopsail
5   Main course
6   Bonnet
7   Main topsail
8   Mizzen course
9   Bonnet

**I1**

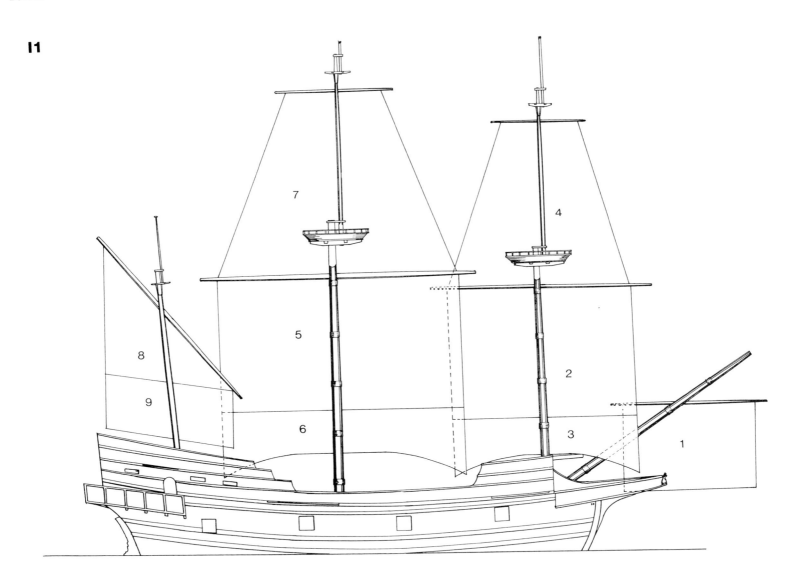

**I2**	**MAINSAIL AND BONNET**
	**(1/96 scale)**
**1**	Fore side
**2**	After side
**3**	Bonnet
**4**	Head rope
**5**	Robband holes
**6**	Tabling
**7**	Head earring
**8**	Martnet cringles
**9**	Leech rope
**10**	Bowline cringles
**11**	Lining
**12**	Holes for lacing
**13**	Footrope
**14**	Clew cringle
**15**	Clew earring

**I2**

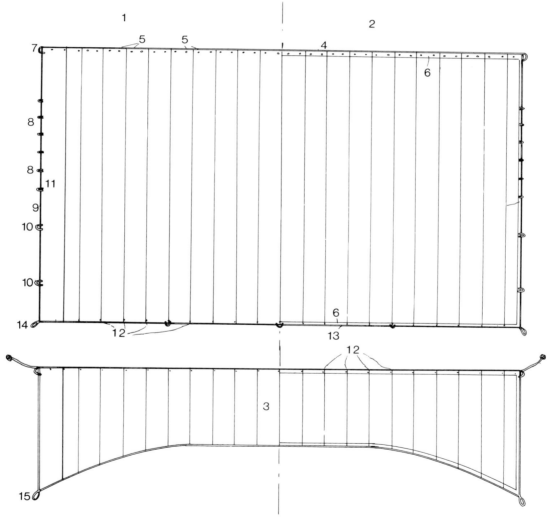

# I  Sails

**I3  MAIN TOPSAIL**
**(1/96 scale)**
1  Fore side
2  After side
3  Bowline cringles
4  Lining
5  Tabling
6  Buntline cringles

**I4  SPRITSAIL**
**(1/96 scale)**
1  Fore side
2  After side
3  Robband holes
4  Tabling
5  Lining
6  Buntline cringle

**I5  MIZZENSAIL AND BONNET**
**(1/96 scale)**
1  Lining
2  Tabling
3  Foot
4  Headrope
5  Leech
6  Robband holes
7  Buntline cringle
8  Holes for bonnet lashing
9  Bonnet
10  Luff

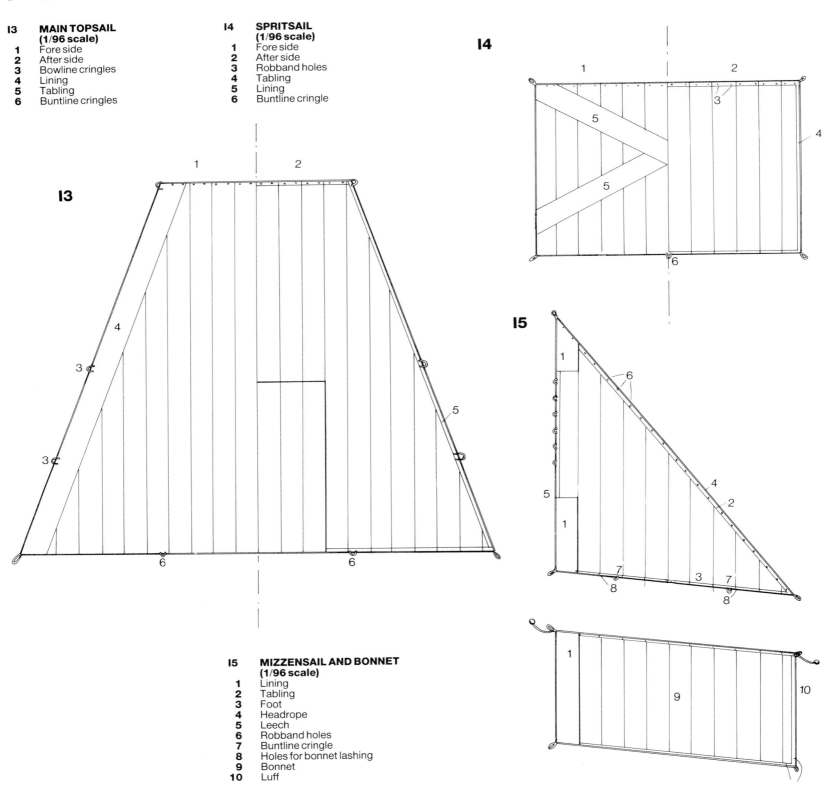

**I6** **POSSIBLE METHOD OF LASHING**
**SAIL TO BONNET**
**(no scale)**
**1** Sail
**2** Bonnet
**3** Holes in bonnet
**4** Holes in sail

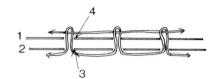

**I7** **FITTING OF SAIL TO YARD**
**(no scale)**
**1** Robbands
**2** Yardarm cleats
**3** Robband holes
**4** Head cringle
**5** Reef knots
**6** Leech rope
**7** Tabling

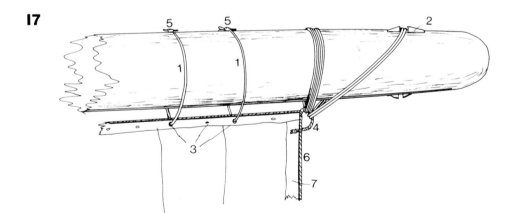

# J Running rigging

**J1 LOWER TIES AND HALYARD**
**(no scale)**

1 Mast head
2 Tie
3 Preventer
4 Ramshead block
5 Halyard
6 Knighthead
7 Eyebolt
8 End of halyard hitched round head
9 Yard

**J2 TOPSAIL HALYARD AND TIE**
**(1/96 scale)**

1 Yard
2 Lift
3 Block
4 Halyard
5 To deck
6 Eyebolt

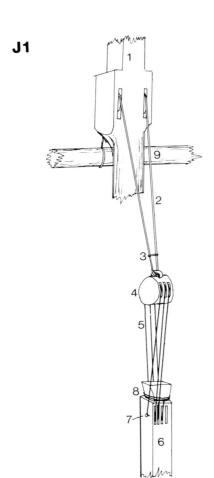

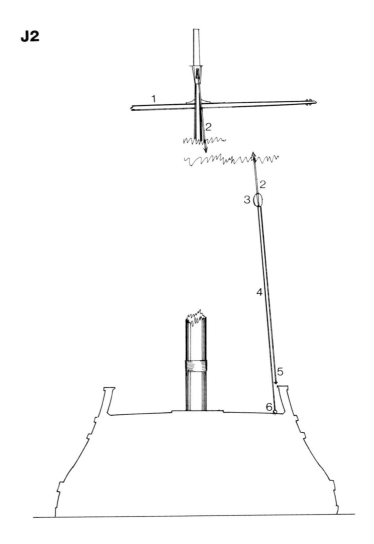

**J3**

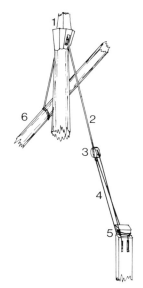

**J5**

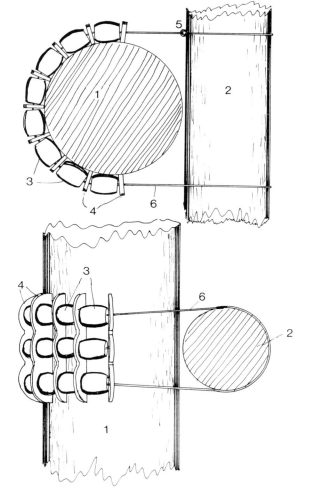

**J4**

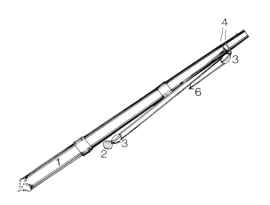

**J6**

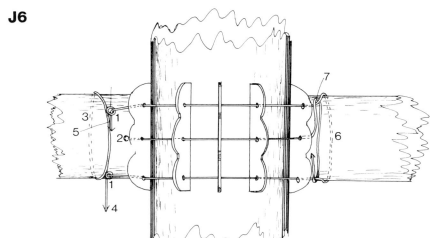

# J  Running rigging

**J7  TIES AND LIFTS OF MAINYARD AND TOPSAIL** (Topsail yard in lowered position) (1/96 scale)

1  Ties
2  Lifts
3  Mainyard
4  Main topsail yard
5  Topsail sheet block
6  Lift block
7  Main lift
8  Mainstay collar
9  Truss

**J8  LIFTS AND BOWLINES OF MIZZEN** (1/192 scale)

1  Lift
2  Bowline
3  After main shroud
4  Blocks
5  To deck

**J9  SPRITSAIL LIFTS** (1/96 scale)

1  Lift
2  Block
3  Spritsail yard
4  Bowsprit
5  To foredeck

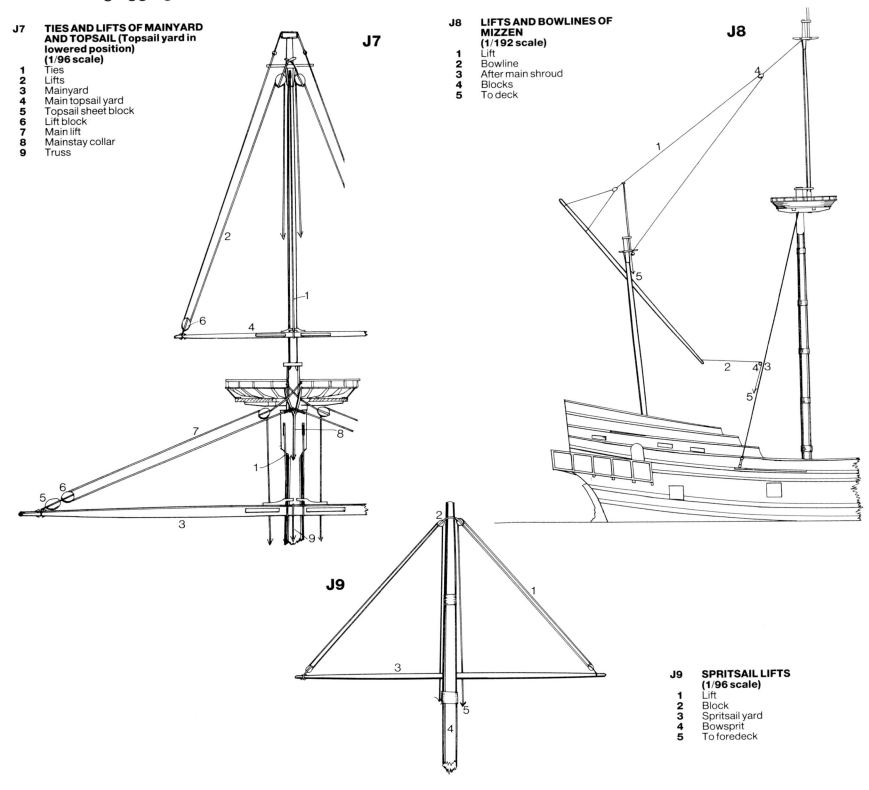

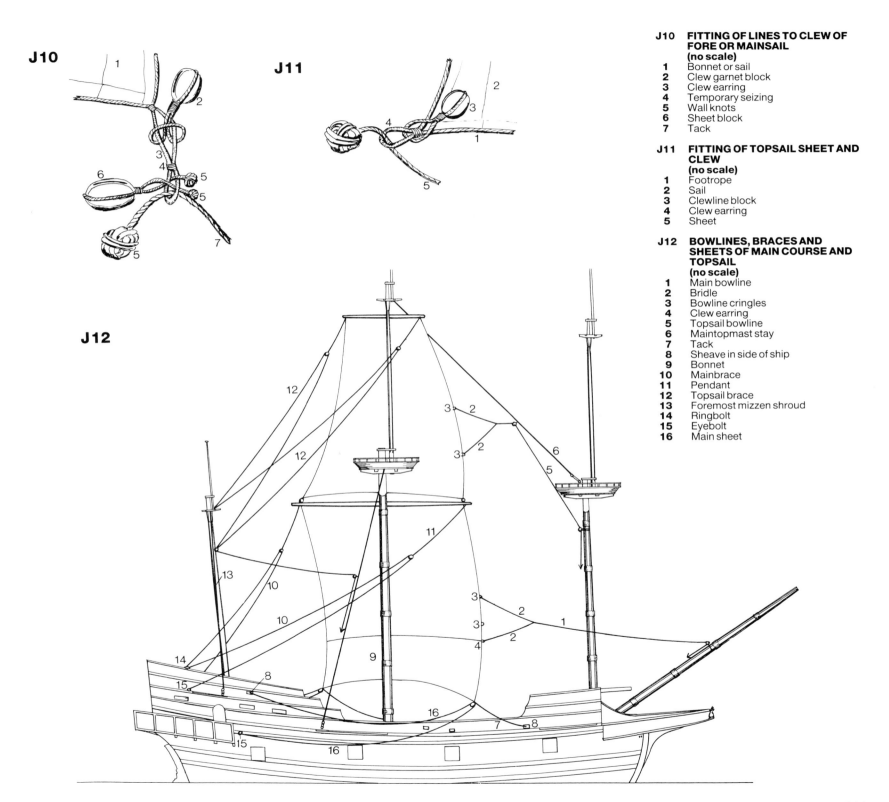

**J10**

**J11**

**J12**

**J10 FITTING OF LINES TO CLEW OF FORE OR MAINSAIL**
(no scale)
1 Bonnet or sail
2 Clew garnet block
3 Clew earring
4 Temporary seizing
5 Wall knots
6 Sheet block
7 Tack

**J11 FITTING OF TOPSAIL SHEET AND CLEW**
(no scale)
1 Footrope
2 Sail
3 Clewline block
4 Clew earring
5 Sheet

**J12 BOWLINES, BRACES AND SHEETS OF MAIN COURSE AND TOPSAIL**
(no scale)
1 Main bowline
2 Bridle
3 Bowline cringles
4 Clew earring
5 Topsail bowline
6 Maintopmast stay
7 Tack
8 Sheave in side of ship
9 Bonnet
10 Mainbrace
11 Pendant
12 Topsail brace
13 Foremost mizzen shroud
14 Ringbolt
15 Eyebolt
16 Main sheet

111

# J  Running rigging

**J13  FOREBRACES, SHEETS AND BOWLINES**
**(1/192 scale)**

1  Foretopmast stay
2  Bowline
3  Bridle
4  To deck
5  Forebrace
6  Pendant
7  Mainstay
8  To side
9  To deck
10  Topsail brace
11  Maintopmast stay
12  Foresheet
13  Tack
14  Sheave
15  Hole under knee of head

**J13**

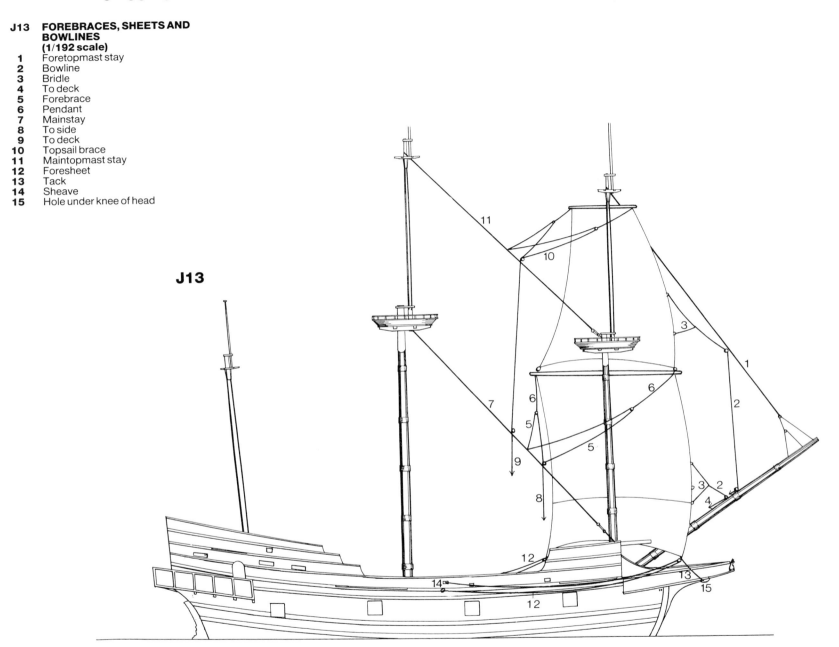

## J14

## J15

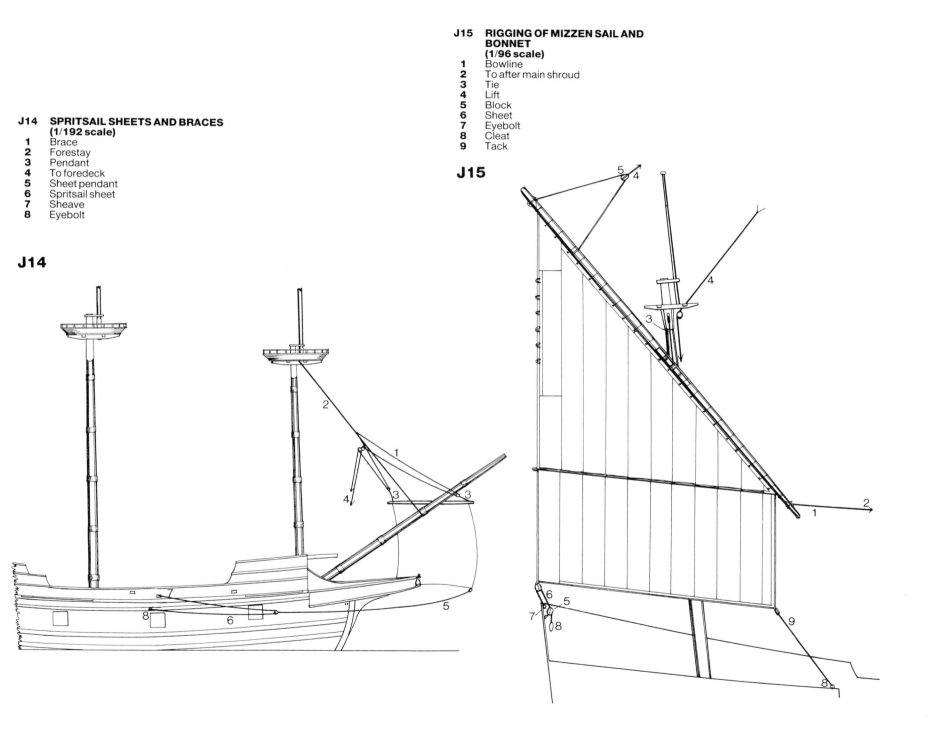

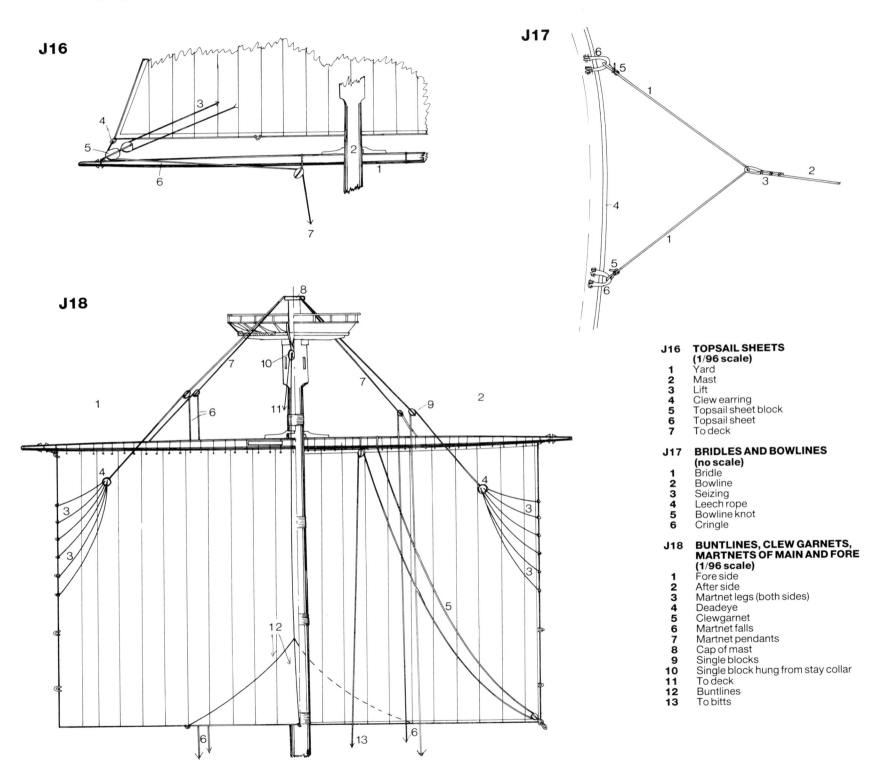

**J16**

**J17**

**J18**

| J16 | **TOPSAIL SHEETS**<br>**(1/96 scale)** |
|---|---|
| 1 | Yard |
| 2 | Mast |
| 3 | Lift |
| 4 | Clew earring |
| 5 | Topsail sheet block |
| 6 | Topsail sheet |
| 7 | To deck |

| J17 | **BRIDLES AND BOWLINES**<br>**(no scale)** |
|---|---|
| 1 | Bridle |
| 2 | Bowline |
| 3 | Seizing |
| 4 | Leech rope |
| 5 | Bowline knot |
| 6 | Cringle |

| J18 | **BUNTLINES, CLEW GARNETS,**<br>**MARTNETS OF MAIN AND FORE**<br>**(1/96 scale)** |
|---|---|
| 1 | Fore side |
| 2 | After side |
| 3 | Martnet legs (both sides) |
| 4 | Deadeye |
| 5 | Clewgarnet |
| 6 | Martnet falls |
| 7 | Martnet pendants |
| 8 | Cap of mast |
| 9 | Single blocks |
| 10 | Single block hung from stay collar |
| 11 | To deck |
| 12 | Buntlines |
| 13 | To bitts |

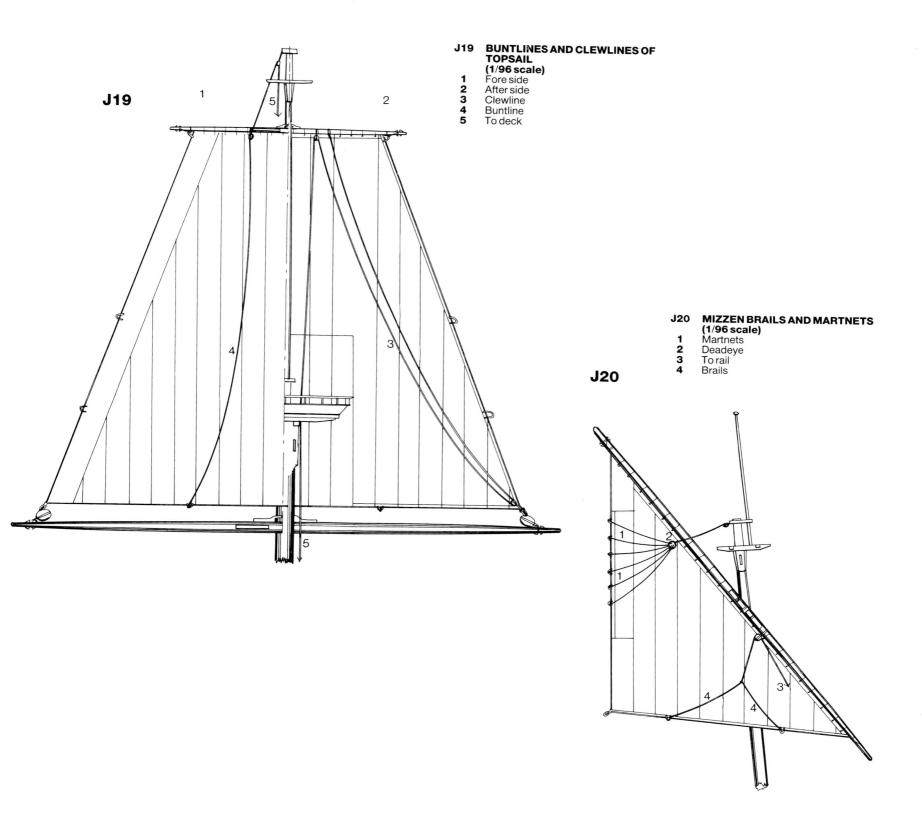

**J19** **BUNTLINES AND CLEWLINES OF**
      **TOPSAIL**
      **(1/96 scale)**
   **1** Fore side
   **2** After side
   **3** Clewline
   **4** Buntline
   **5** To deck

**J20** **MIZZEN BRAILS AND MARTNETS**
      **(1/96 scale)**
   **1** Martnets
   **2** Deadeye
   **3** To rail
   **4** Brails

115

# J  Running rigging

## J21  BUNTLINES AND CLEW LINES OF SPRITSAIL (1/96 scale)

1  Bowsprit
2  Block
3  Buntline
4  To foredeck
5  Clewline
6  Sail
7  Spritsail yard

## J22  LEAD OF ROPES THROUGH GAMMONING BLOCK (port side similar, but no foretopmast stay) (1/96 scale)

1  Forward rail of foredeck
2  Gammoning
3  Gammoning block
4  Foretopmast stay
5  Foretopsail bowline
6  Main bowline
7  Fore bowline

**J21**

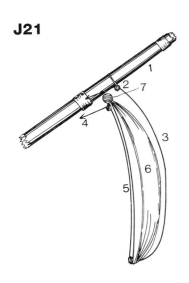

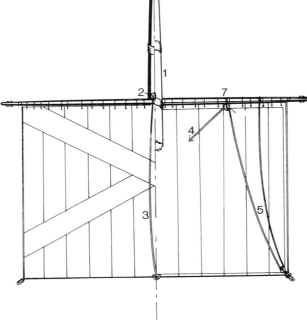

**J22**

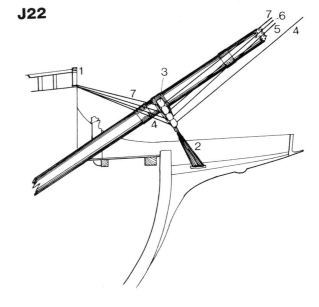

## J23  FORECASTLE RANGE (1/48 scale)

1  Knighthead
2  Pins
3  Crossbar
4  Sheaves
5  Forecastle deck beams

## J24  TYPES OF KEVEL (no scale)

1  Single kevel with rope in groove underneath
2  Single kevel with sheave
3  Double kevel
4  Sheave in side

## J25  CLEAT ON MAST (no scale)

## J26  HEAD ON KNIGHTHEAD (no scale)

**J25**

**J24**

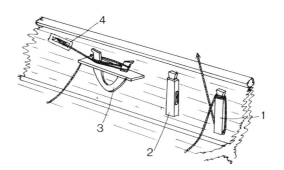

**J23**

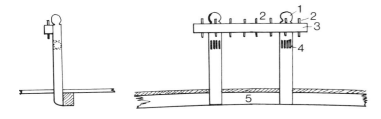

**J26**

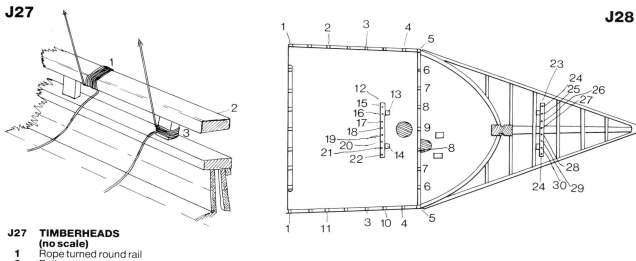

## J27

**J27 TIMBERHEADS**
**(no scale)**
1 Rope turned round rail
2 Rail
3 Rope turned round timberhead

## J28

## J29

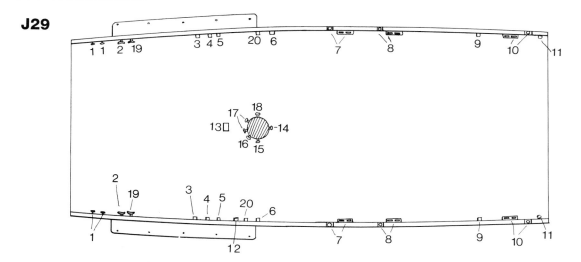

## J30

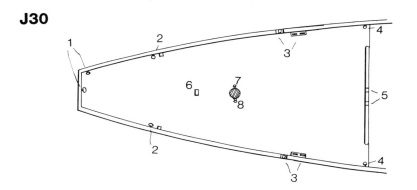

# K  Armament

**K1  MINION, 7ft LONG**
**(1/24 scale)**
1  Trunnions
2  Cascabel
3  Swell of muzzle
4  Touch hole
5  Bore

**K3  MINION CARRIAGE, PROFILE**
**(1/24 scale)**
1  Capsquare
2  Quoins
3  Ringbolts
4  Transom
5  Lynchpin
6  Truck
7  Bed
8  Axle

**K1**

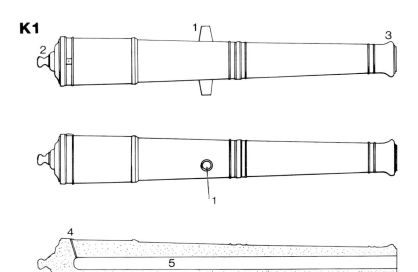

**K3**

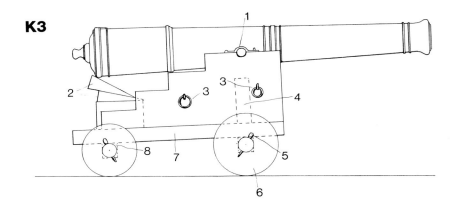

**K4**

**K2  FALCON, 7ft LONG**
**(1/24 scale)**

**K2**

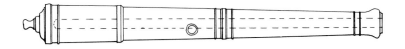

**K4  MINION CARRIAGE, PLAN**
**(1/24 scale)**
1  Capsquare
2  Transom
3  Bed
4  Bracket
5  Truck
6  Ringbolt

**K5**    **FALCON CARRIAGE, PROFILE**
        **(1/24 scale)**

**K6**    **FALCON CARRIAGE, PLAN**
        **(1/24 scale)**

**K7**    **MINION IN NORMAL AND FIRING**
        **POSITION**
        **(1/24 scale)**
        Gun tackle

## K5

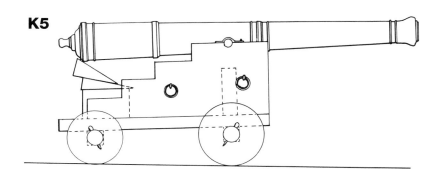

## K7

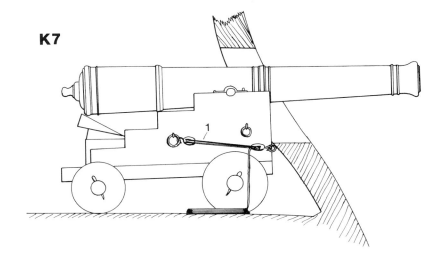

## K 6

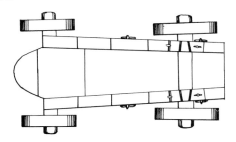

**K8**    **MINION LASHED FOR HEAVY**
        **WEATHER**
        **(1/24 scale)**

| | |
|---|---|
| **1** | Breeching |
| **2** | Lashing |
| **3** | Gun tackle |
| **4** | Single block |
| **5** | Double block |
| **6** | Knot |
| **7** | Port lid |
| **8** | Quoins |

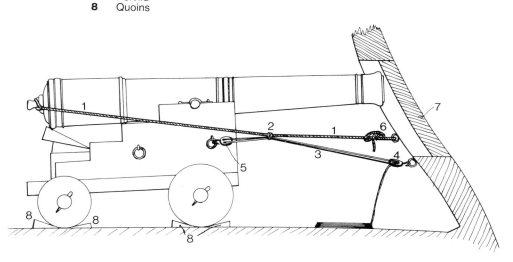

## K8

# K Armament

**K9** **RINGBOLTS FOR GUN AND BREECH TACKLE, ON SIDE OF SHIP**
**(1/24 scale)**
1 Gunport
2 Ringbolts for breech rope
3 Ringbolts for gun tackle
4 Waterway

**K10** **FITTING OF BREECH ROPE TO CASCABEL**
**(1/12 scale)**
1 Cascabel
2 Breech
3 Breech rope
4 Seizing

## K9

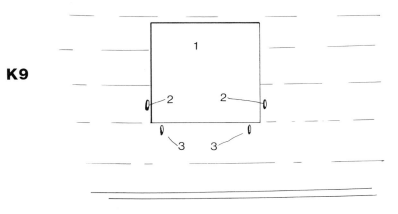

## K10

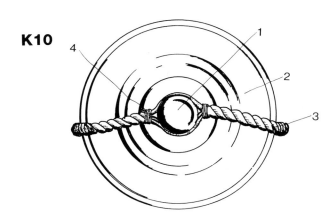

**K11** **CROSS-SECTION OF CLOSED GUNPORT**
**(1/24 scale)**
1 Hole in side
2 Port tackle
3 Hinge
4 Nails for hinge
5 Ringbolt
6 Eyebolt

**K12** **OPENING OF GUNPORT**
**(1/24 scale)**

**K13** **GUNPORT LID**
**(1/24 scale)**
1 From outside
2 From inside

## K11

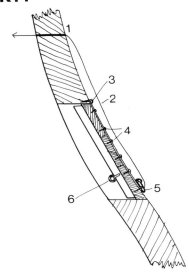

## K12

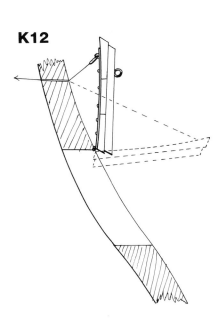

## K13

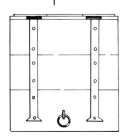
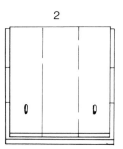